MY TURN AT THE BULLY PULPIT

MY TURN
AT THE
BULLY PULPIT

STRAIGHT TALK ABOUT THE THINGS
THAT DRIVE ME NUTS

GRETA VAN SUSTEREN
AND ELAINE LAFFERTY

Crown Publishers / New York

Published by Crown Publishers, New York, New York.
Member of the Crown Publishing Group, a division of Random House, Inc.
www.randomhouse.com

CROWN is a trademark and the Crown colophon is a registered trademark of Random House, Inc.

Printed in the United States of America

Design by Leonard Henderson

Library of Congress Cataloging-in-Publication Data
Van Susteren, Greta
    My turn at the bully pulpit : straight talk about the things that drive me nuts / by Greta Van Susteren and Elaine Lafferty.—1st ed.
        p. cm.
    1. Law—United States—Anecdotes. 2. Lawyers on television—United States—Anecdotes. 3. Women television personalities—United States—Anecdotes. I. Lafferty, Elaine. II. Title.
K184.V36 2003
349.73—dc21

                                                                2003007601

ISBN 1-4000-4662-9

10 9 8 7 6 5 4 3 2 1

For John Coale, my husband and very best friend

Acknowledgments

As you might imagine, you don't get to my age with such great jobs and fascinating projects without *lots* of help from many people. To avoid the problem of forgetting someone, and to avoid the bigger problem of having the complete acknowledgment exceed the text, I single out a very few. This is not to suggest that there are not literally hundreds whose names should appear here. I have had a lot of help during my life—help that ultimately appears in some form in my life and thus in the following pages.

Gail Evans, the former executive vice president of CNN, called me in 1991 to do legal analysis on CNN. She gave me the proverbial "chance." I remained at CNN until the end of 2001. Gail saw something in me that I never saw or thought. *Who would have thought I could do TV!!* I remain indebted to Gail for always helping me and forever shepherding me through the perilous waters of twenty-four-hour cable news. She has placed enormous faith in me and in my career and I hope I have not disappointed her.

I am grateful to the chairman and CEO of Fox News, Roger Ailes—not just for hiring me but for his loyalty to all his employees. He has made it fun to work at Fox. We know we can depend on him. That makes a huge difference to how we work and how we look at our work. It makes coming to work each day anything but "work."

The "cabal"—those intimately involved with putting the book together—deserves great thanks from me. My coauthor, Elaine Lafferty, is not only a skilled writer able to capture my voice, but has shown enormous patience with me (more than I would have shown if I had been in her shoes). She also gets all the credit for the stuff you like in the book. Most importantly, Elaine is a damn good friend and in my mind, there is no higher compliment.

Bia Lowe is our behind the scenes help, who by trade is a serious literary writer but who I may have sufficiently corrupted to the point that she can now name the Green Bay Packers.

Our editor, Annik LaFarge, has been inspiring—besides giving us the guidance we needed at every step, she understood from the very beginning that this project had to be fun. I much appreciated her careful comments about every page as the project moved through each phase—including those comments that essentially said, "This makes no sense."

David Black, our literary agent, brought to the table a vision of what this book should be and could be. He defines the role of literary agent quite broadly, which means he rolled up his sleeves and helped far beyond what I had expected.

Nicole Rogers, my assistant, was, as is her habit, willing to do anything to help, and she did. Someday, I know she will have my job. (And she deserves it!)

Finally—John, my husband. He has never stopped helping me on every project for more than twenty-three years. He is the smartest person I know (and the most fun).

—*Greta*

Acknowledgments

I WAS STANDING ON THE BALCONY OF a run-down house in Kabul, covering the conflict in Afghanistan, when the voice on the other end of the satellite phone became adamant. "I want to do this book and I want you to help me!" said Greta. I told her I wasn't sure I could, that I was writing about Al Qaeda, the dire situation of women under the Taliban, that sort of thing. Greta, who exhibits in my view an unreasonable aversion to having her friends ensconced in war zones, was, however, persuasive in her usual sophisticated and logical fashion. "Come back here to do this book or I will have you committed."

My deepest gratitude, then, is to Greta. Anyone who has ever worked with her knows that her intelligence, integrity, and energy make her a joy. Anyone who has ever worked with her is now trying to get some sleep.

Many thanks to the friends whose suggestions, edits, advice, and support were invaluable; Bia Lowe, Barbara Pepe, Shelly Mandell, Kim Masters, and Peter Murtagh.

David Black is far more than an agent. Not only the smartest in the business, but a dearly kind and generous man as well. Our editor, Annik LaFarge, who is both brilliant and patient, will someday run the world.

Finally, to everyone at *Ms.* magazine and its publishers, the Feminist Majority, most especially Eleanor Smeal and Peg Yorkin. A special thanks to Sarah Gonzales.

Oh yeah, one more person: Mr. John Coale. Many thanks. Any more bright ideas?

—Elaine

Contents

MY TURN AT THE BULLY PULPIT

Foreword and Forewarned

Let me tell you what this book is . . . and what it is not. I hope you are still standing in the bookstore as you read this and can decide whether to buy it or not! This book represents my take on issues, large and small—what I think about, and how I came to think it. This book is not a scholarly text aimed at analyzing and deconstructing the issues facing America today. It's not an academic treatise. You are simply going to find out what I think at this moment and why I think it, based on how I have lived my life, both personally and professionally. My view of the world and of the critical issues facing us is based on what I have seen and what I have learned—in my law practice, through my life experiences, and in my career as a legal and news analyst on television.

I grew up in the Midwest, and I fundamentally remain a midwesterner at heart even though I have lived in Washington, D.C., for most of my adult life. I was born in 1954, meaning that my formative years were in the 1960s and 1970s, a tumultuous time in America. While I am of the generation that was considered part of the backbone of 1960s radicalism and liberalism, the fact is that my essential political views and moral values were formed much more by midwestern Catholic middle-class sensibilities than those of someone who grew up on the East or West Coast and went to elite schools. I attended neither Harvard nor Berkeley, but the good old University of Wisconsin at Madison.

I recently had lunch with Henry Kissinger, who is a frequent guest on my show. I sat there thinking how unimaginable it would have been for most of my life that I'd be sharing a meal with someone who is inarguably, no matter how you feel about him, one of the most important figures in modern American history. We began discussing war, and the conversation turned to the anti–Vietnam War demonstrations that shook this country during the time Kissinger served in the Nixon White House. I told Kissinger that indeed I had attended some of those demonstrations as a teenager. He became silent. The Vietnam War demonstrations were some of the most emotional and divisive moments in American history. It was apparent that Dr. Kissinger remembered them clearly.

"Well, beyond everything else, they were the best parties in town," I said. "I don't think some of us in our early teens knew where Vietnam was, and I didn't even know whose side the Viet Cong were on!" We laughed. My point was not to defend or explain my position on the Vietnam War, nor to reargue the matter or reopen anyone's old wounds, including his. The point was simply this: Vietnam was a long time ago, and as with so many other controversial and painful aspects of American history, we must live in the present and move on from old hurts.

I also do not intend to demean or represent the millions of Americans who did demonstrate against the war and were seriously and deeply informed. My then attitude toward Vietnam and demonstrations was the utter naiveté of youth. I was a teenager at the time. I was still in high school. What I do mean to say is that history is sometimes not all it seems, and time brings perspective. Some of us, and I include myself, had no idea what we were actually protesting. In truth, I've become a little bit more informed since then and picked up more than my share of degrees and academic credentials. Yet still, what I truly know and believe was formed at home and in the trenches of life. Frankly, I find books that are no more than someone's rabid opinions larded with 67 pages of footnotes that refer to clips pulled from the *New York Times* and the wire services completely bogus. The footnotes are meant to make the work look scholarly, but when you scrape the surface, all you're getting is one person's view—maybe an educated and informed one, but still a single opinion.

Our country is at a critical juncture. I believe that too many of us are caught up in old definitions of left and right that no longer apply. If I favor the death penalty in some cases, does that make me right-wing? If I think hate crimes legislation is unnecessary because of existing laws, does that make me a conservative? If I happen to like and enjoy Ozzy Osbourne and have him on my show, does that make me a liberal? And if I believe that corporations should be held accountable and subject to the rulings of a jury if their products harm citizens—ditto for doctors who commit medical malpractice—does that make me a lefty trial lawyer?

You see, I believe these definitions may have been valid at one time. But they rarely apply anymore, except for the most extreme elements of our society. Fundamentally, I believe, we all want the same things: freedom, liberty, equal opportunity for all based on merit and hard work. I believe most of us oppose discrimination. We are more than willing to pay taxes provided the government fulfills its end of the contract. We want clean streets, safe schools, a decent and fair health care system. So what do we fight about? Well, I guess many of us have different ideas about strategy, about how to accomplish our common goals. But the fact that we *do* have common goals is an extraordinary thing when you stop to think about it. Having such shared goals distinguishes us from so many countries in the world. We differ on strategies to achieve them, that's all! Do you realize how amazing and unique that makes us? I may favor the right of a woman to choose to have an abortion in consultation with her doctor, but I also recognize the legitimacy of a different point of view. But don't we both agree that children should be entitled to safety, security, and a decent education?

So go ahead and read this book. The views are all mine; the mistakes and wrongheaded illogic are all my coauthor's. (Just kidding!) But that leads me to another theme you'll find peppered throughout this book: having fun, something I try to do as often as possible both at work and at home. Because the truth is that we all need to lighten up a bit, at least from time to time. So in this book you'll find the serious issues but also some not-so-serious ones. I do hope you have some fun reading it.

1

ANATOMY OF A CABLE NEWS SHOW: GETTING RATINGS AND GETTING THE "GET"

Television news shouldn't be boring, and doesn't need to be. Engaging the viewer is not "dumbing down"! Competition is a good thing.

WINNING THE RATINGS WAR

EVERY AFTERNOON I DO SOMETHING THAT most people in television news say they don't do. I look at the ratings from the night before. I sit at my desk with these Excel spreadsheets laid out before me, and I immerse myself in the business of television ratings, studying who watches, when, why, and how.

Why do some people in TV deny they do this? Even stranger, maybe these people are not fudging—maybe they're telling the truth and they actually never do sneak a peak. To listen to them, you'd think that monitoring ratings is somehow degrading, that it sullies their hands to actually care whether viewers are tuned in.

Not me. I'm competitive; I need and like to have a method of keeping score. I want to win my time slot, to beat out the competition, and I also care about my viewers and don't want to put them to sleep! What's wrong with that? It's no compromise of integrity, journalistic or otherwise, to keep my audience engaged. There is nothing wrong with wanting people to watch your show if you are on television! It's my duty and also my privilege.

How do I know if I'm doing a good job or not unless I have some score to examine? I use my ratings to figure out what it is the viewers want and respond to. Believe me, it doesn't feel good when the ratings go down, but it does give me the opportunity to evaluate: What didn't work? What could I have done differently? How can I improve? The law is a service industry, and so is television—or at least it should be.

Ratings are upped when viewers tune in and stay tuned in, and it feels like a stamp of approval. Getting great ratings is fun, like winning a race, but it's also rewarding. It means that the product I worked hard on all day long was a good one. Viewers voted!

It's a big fat lie when people in the news business claim, "I don't care about ratings." When someone declares himself indifferent to ratings, it's a good indication he's just lost the ratings war. It's as transparent as a kid who can't dribble a basketball and pouts, "Basketball is dumb!" The folks at CNN may deny they're concerned about ratings, that they're above competition and focused solely on great journalism, but that's hard to believe when they spend $15 million to build Paula Zahn a new set! I think their sudden change of heart about ratings began in 2002, when Fox became the number one cable news network.

Ignoring ratings may also suggest extreme arrogance. People in television should care whether the viewers are pleased with the presentation. To ignore ratings and to simply program a show with what the anchor wants means the anchor has decided what the viewer should watch.

This isn't to suggest that people in the news business should be so spellbound by ratings as to lose all good judgment and moral commitment. But how we package the news is important, and it doesn't require us to compromise integrity.

GRABBING AND KEEPING
THE VIEWER'S ATTENTION
DOESN'T MEAN DUMBING DOWN

Studying the ratings can tell you a lot—for example, when people start going to sleep. My show is at 10 P.M. Eastern time. By that time of night, sleep is starting to look mighty tempting to a lot of people on the East Coast. Others might be about to pick up the phone to call their mothers, or to order one of those pizzas they see advertised during commercial breaks. My job is to keep everybody awake and locked on Fox! No droopy eyes, no phone calls. Thumbs are not allowed to move on those remotes until eleven o'clock!

Now, it doesn't mean that all I have to do to hold the viewers' attention is to program tabloid subjects or book hot guests. If only it were that easy. If gaining and keeping viewers tuned in was as easy as just programming tabloid subjects all the time, everyone would be doing it and doing it well. Audiences are too savvy for a formula as simple as that.

Our show and many others have gotten good ratings featuring guests who hardly qualify as tabloid material—guests such as Henry Kissinger and former White House chief of staff David Gergen, not to mention the innumerable military and policy analysts who've given their opinions on some very serious, very dry subjects. The point is that you have to engage your guests with the important questions, invite discussion, and make difficult subjects interesting. Involving your viewers is about creating the right mix, staying focused, and keeping the energy high.

How do I make sure I can project energy? It's simple: I make sure *I* stay curious. I am no different from viewers: I don't want to be bored either.

I KEEP LEARNING FROM MY VIEWERS

It can be challenging to guess what will appeal to viewers. It's an ongoing lesson. And here again, the ratings can be very instructive. One time on *Burden of Proof,* the afternoon show I used to do on CNN, a staff member wanted to do a show on Alzheimer's disease. Alzheimer's disease? You have to be kidding. What could be more depressing? How was I going to keep any of my viewers tuned into a show about elderly loved ones dying a slow death? What could be engaging about that kind of heartbreak? I was outvoted by my colleagues, so against my better judgment, we did the show.

Well, the viewers liked it; the ratings were incredible. Okay, maybe *liked* is the wrong word—but they watched it.

Our Alzheimer's show was hardly entertaining; it was a how-to show. We explained how someone should prepare himself and his family legally when the diagnosis is first given. We pursued the course of the disease down its path to the point where the afflicted become legally incompetent. We defined incompetence—what it is, how it is proven, and what happens if the party objects to the proceeding. Our guests had solid experience with the important issues, including a judge who spoke plainly about the problems of establishing legal incompetence. In short, here was a show without celebrity, spin, or sensationalism—just information, pure and simple, none of which was "pretty" or would win us a popularity contest—but the viewers tuned in and stayed tuned in.

GETTING THE "GET"

Everybody in the news business knows about the "get." One of the most talked-about things inside the television business is what some people will do to get an interview. The stories are legend— and for that reason I can't repeat them here because I simply don't know which ones are true or exaggerated—but take it from me, you hear the gamut, from bribery to blondes.

The "get" is someone at the center of a big story. The "get" is the guest everybody has to have at that moment. It can be a celebrity or someone who by circumstance simply happens to be in the vortex of a major news story. In short, the "get" is to news what prey is to predator.

One journalist I know calls that moment when every reporter is in a frenzy over a story the "get-the-mother" moment. It's macabre, but whenever there's a major news story about a child in this country (and these days, sadly, it's usually a tragic one), you can almost hear the top editors and producers across the United States yelling at their reporters to go out there and get the woman who's at the heart of it.

We can be critical of the practice of "getting the mother," but in fact sought-after interviewees are sought after for one good and simple reason: They know something. They can shed light on the story; they can *explain*. Viewers want to hear from people close to the center of a story, and who can blame them? Likewise, I don't want to watch a bunch of droning talking heads who are unrelated to the topic or simply uninformed.

THE FRENZY TURNS FICKLE

Of course, the best "get" is the person who is the subject of the story. In times of war, that might be the U.S. president and the secretaries of defense and state. The president of the opposing country would be in this category too.

But oh, how things can change. If a pilot gets shot down during a war and is rescued, he and his heroic rescuers immediately trump the president and the secretaries. Everyone warms to a human-interest story, and war issues pale next to coverage of flesh-and-blood heroes in life-threatening circumstances. It will quickly become "President who?" The pilot and his rescuers bolt to the top of the bookers' "get" list. The chase is on. You can practically smell the adrenaline. You should hear the discussions: "Does anyone know anyone who went to high school with any of these rescuers? How about the pilot?" Or "Wait—I was in Girl Scouts with the pilot's brother's wife." Or "A friend of a friend knows his dentist." It can get pretty silly. But few leads are left unpursued because sometimes—who knows—it may work.

But then the inevitable happens: Once the pilot and his heroic rescuers have made the circuit of all the talk shows, they begin to vanish from the list. They become, unfortunately, yesterday's news, on the floor of the parakeet's cage. Remember old what's-his-name?

Anyone who has ever been courted by reporters and bookers

can be surprised at how fickle the "getting" can be. You could be the subject of the most important news story and be debating with yourself whether to do Katie or Diane, when suddenly a bigger news story hits the street. Suddenly your calls to the producers and bookers are not returned. You may have been flattered by the continuous delivery of flowers to your house, but you can be dropped like a hot potato as soon as something else bumps you from the radar screen.

This isn't to suggest that the media intend to be rude, but journalists operate on a fast track of breaking news. It is not sentimental and it is not especially kind. We move very quickly between news stories—and always at an unpredictable pace. Planning for a future story is a fantasy, because as soon as a new story "happens" we drop everything for the next big thing on the wire.

And, of course, being a "get" can also get you what you want, provided you play your cards right. For instance, during the controversy over Senator Trent Lott's birthday cheer for Senator Strom Thurmond, Lott was the "get" to get. Viewers wanted to know the story behind Lott's remarks. What could the senator have been thinking when he made those comments about the country being better off if Senator Thurmond had won the presidency in 1948? Didn't he realize those words would be perceived as racist?

It was in Mr. Lott's interest to clear some things up, to restore his reputation, and he had a specific audience he wanted to address. The prize for the "get" went to BET (Black Entertainment Television). Even the *Today* show and *Good Morning America* were left in the dust. But the getting, in this instance, was mutually beneficial.

I hate to be so presumptuous as to state why a potential "get" chooses one show over another, but I do have a pretty good idea what goes into the decision. I learned firsthand when I myself became the "get." (Remember the media frenzy after my plastic surgery? See Chapter 6 for more on that.) I've also been in competition with other shows and been told what the competitor's pitch was.

Let me give you an insight into how this competition works. I should add that I hope you are never the subject of a major news story, as it is usually bad news (unless you win the lottery).

First the bookers inform the "get" of the channel's or network's ratings. "You will reach more people this way" is a very powerful argument to people looking for a missing child or for someone who has an ideological point to make. The networks are at a huge advantage, since network TV is free to anyone who has a television. Cable is in fewer homes, as many people can't get access to cable or can't afford it. (CNN is in more homes. But at least as I write this, Fox is seen by more viewers.) So Fox and CNN have to compete with the networks in a different way, because we in cable don't have the huge number of homes that the networks do. But we have something they do not: time. As a result, we can carpet-bomb the airwaves with interviews. Sound bites and the interview can play 24/7. The networks have very limited airtime devoted to their interviews. We can replay the interviews multiple times and in so doing raise the number of viewers who can see it. This is not to say that ratings are the *only* method of getting the "get." The credibility of the host may play a significant role, or the "get" may be particularly fond of an anchor. Sometimes bookers and producers build up a rapport with a potential interviewee, and that person goes on gut instinct or loyalty to a perceived new friend. I frequently have an advantage in legal matters since I am a lawyer and other lawyers often feel comfortable talking to me. It makes sense, since I'm in the club. But sometimes being a lawyer is irrelevant or even a drawback. Some guests have confessed to me that they were afraid to go on with me, thinking my being a lawyer would translate into me hammering them rudely on television. They soon find out: I can be tough, but I try never to be rude.

SOMETIMES COMPETITION HAS A PRICE

Sometimes you can find yourself in competition for the "get" without even knowing it. In one sad instance I walked into a competition for a guest without realizing it, and it destroyed a new friendship. Here is what happened:

In July 2001 Sharon Osbourne was diagnosed with cancer. I received a call telling me about it two nights before Ozzy and Sharon were supposed to be in Washington, D.C., and scheduled to attend a small party at my house. The party had been an afterthought—the reason for their trip to Washington was that Ozzy was to perform at Ozzfest that week. With the diagnosis, the concert and of course the party were canceled.

About four weeks later, Ozzfest was rescheduled for the Washington area. Because Sharon was receiving treatments for her cancer, Ozzy traveled alone.

I like Ozzy very much. My husband, John Coale, and I hadn't seen him since the White House correspondents' dinner, and I thought it would be fun to do a short interview with him, a change of pace from regular news. Ozzy and his family had come to redefine family values, real commitment, and love without sugar coating. He and Sharon are fun, and John and I are fond of them both.

Fox put in the call and asked if Ozzy wanted to do it. His assistant asked what topic, and my assistant responded that I didn't care—whatever Ozzy wanted to talk about. Offhand, I even suggested we talk about Elvis Presley, since it was the anniversary of his death and I figured Ozzy had lots to say about the King.

Ozzie agreed to the interview, and the next day John, the crew, and I were at his hotel. John went to Ozzy's room to say hello, and I went to the suite where our cameras were set up. John and I had talked about Sharon earlier, and we were worried about her and about Ozzy. We figured that Ozzy was very upset, and we just wanted to be nice to him and take the lead from him should he say something. We saw this as part of our friendship, separate and apart from my job.

John walked into Ozzy's room and said, "How's the queen?" He meant Queen Elizabeth, since Ozzy had recently returned from England, where he'd entertained the queen at her jubilee. But Ozzy thought John meant Sharon, and he started talking nonstop about how upset he was about her. Of course John let him talk.

Moments later Ozzy came down the hall to the suite where I was with all the cameras set up. When he walked in the room I gave him a hug. We then sat down before the cameras, and the first thing I said was "How are you?" With that Ozzy continued talking very candidly about Sharon. Of course, I had no idea at the time that he had been pouring his heart out to John. I just let him talk, since he obviously wanted to. At one point Ozzy said on camera, "I need to talk about this." I certainly wasn't going to stop the outpouring. It was touching, loving, and vulnerable.

The interview ended, and I returned to the bureau with the tape. To give the interview maximum exposure, we decided to air a portion of it first on Fox's magazine show *The Pulse* and then to air it in its entirety the following night on my show, *On the Record*.

But a day or two later, before the interview aired, something disturbing happened. I was in New York in a cab on my way to the airport and called my voice mail. I had a message from a woman who identified herself as the Osbornes' attorney.

I called her, and she started quizzing me about the interview. I told her all about it, as there was nothing to hide. I was proud of it—it was a great interview. I thought she was satisfied, but I admit I thought it weird that she had me on speakerphone. I figured she was inexperienced and trying to show off, so I just let her do it. I have a dim view of lawyers who insist on using speakerphones to flex their muscles. Frankly, they seem weak and stupid to me, but that's for another book.

The next day she called again. This time she was plain threatening. She told me that I hadn't gotten permission to do the interview.

I hadn't gotten permission? *What is with this woman?* I thought. *Is she nuts?* Of course I had permission. What did she think, that I tied Ozzy down and forced him to talk? And why the fury, since the interview was 100 percent positive? Did she really believe that I would be cowed by threats? This was about the silliest legal flailing I'd ever heard.

I figured she was a young attorney with little experience. She was so out of her league that I asked her, "Have you spoken to Ozzy about the interview?" She said no. I then said, "Have you ever met your client?" and she said no. Then I knew she was a lap-dog for someone. With some disdain I recommended she meet and actually speak to her client and get the facts straight before she makes calls. This is elementary.

The next day I was handed a letter from a law firm threatening to get an injunction against Fox airing the interview, and saying the clients would seek monetary damages. It was preposterous. Of course it was ignored.

I assumed after the interview aired and the dust from this mix-up had cleared, that Ozzy and Sharon and I would talk. I couldn't imagine that they actually didn't want the interview broadcast or why there would be legal threats. We were friendly—we didn't need lawyers to speak on our behalf. So about two weeks later, to break the ice, I sent flowers to their home and asked if we could talk, but I never got a reply.

What happened? I don't know. I hope, since there was obviously no legal ground supporting their threats, that these lawyers did not bill the Osbornes for their "legal work." I might add that no lawsuit was ever filed. At least the lawyers got smarter as time passed, but they destroyed a friendship.

Not too long after the interview aired, I read in the paper that Barbara Walters was promoting an "exclusive" with Sharon Osbourne—the first interview since Sharon was diagnosed. I later was told via the grapevine that my interview with Ozzy and his long discussion about Sharon's health had "stepped on the toes" of Barbara Walters' interview, which was intended to be an exclusive.

Frankly, I wish someone had just been straight with me. At this point I hold no grudges with the Osbornes, and I still think their lawyers should be ashamed of themselves. As for Barbara Walters, her ratings were astronomical that night. She is still the best competition in the business. No one gets her "get" like Barbara.

GETTING A CONTROVERSIAL "GET"

O.J. Simpson told me that when he got out of jail after his acquittal he received flowers and chocolates from many of the big honchos in TV news. At the time I was new to the business and was surprised at the big names: *Wow, he got flowers from her?* The list of people who sent him solicitations was the who's who of the media. They all attempted to ingratiate themselves in the hope he'd select one from the list for an exclusive interview. He was, at the time, the "get" to get.

But O.J. Simpson gave his first interview to me—without conditions. I was able to ask him anything I wanted, and no money was paid to him.

A quick digression here: I did not pursue a Simpson interview. At the time I did not think I could get it. Instead O.J. Simpson called me right after he was found not guilty and released from jail. I was stunned to get the call out of the blue.

Of course, the second I heard his voice, I wanted to figure out a way to get the "get." As everyone who knows Simpson is aware, he talks, talks, talks, and talks. That day was no exception. I listened to him for about forty-five minutes straight before I realized that I was late to pick up John at an airport an hour away.

I also did not want to lose the chance at the interview. So I decided to continue the conversation from the car. I broke into his monologue and said, "O.J., can I have your phone number to call you back? I have to go pick up my husband, and if I'm late, he'll *kill* me."

No sooner were the words out of my mouth than I realized what I had just said. I nearly fell over, but it was too late to stop the poor choice of words.

I said, "I am so sorry." He astounded me by responding, "That's okay. People do that often."

After I got the interview, some of the big TV names—the ones who had been sending flowers—claimed not to have wanted the interview. Some said they wouldn't have done it even if Simpson himself had called and begged. Oh, please! What was the point of the flowers and chocolates? A welcome-home gift? I don't think so.

Sure, he was considered a social outcast and a murderer by many, but the news business is about wooing and interviewing newsmakers. Don't forget, there have been interviews of Charles Manson and Saddam Hussein. It didn't mean the anchor or network endorsed that person's conduct. People are curious about what someone in the news has to say, what makes him or her tick. I'm no different; I like to know too. I am curious. That's what makes great television.

The Simpson interview generated controversy and was widely watched. News, like criminal trials, is rarely "pretty." You know what news is for the most part—war, nuclear threats, missing persons, plane crashes, and so on. News is controversy, danger, and tragedy. Rarely is any of it warm and fuzzy. The best you can hope for is a moment of insight, something that makes you think, that keeps you engaged.

MY FAVORITE GUESTS

My hierarchy of guests to book is this: First, I want the players. I want someone with firsthand knowledge. I want someone "in it," right in the middle of the story. That is common sense.

My second choice is someone who actually knows the players or is a witness to the news. Again, this is common sense.

My third choice—and this is important—is someone who is smart. Viewers are not stupid. They demand smart guests, and they can tell the difference. Plus, smart guests make my job easy. And when I say smart, I don't mean full of formal education. Formal education does not measure someone's intelligence (it could just mean your parents had enough money to keep you in school for a long time). No, I mean native intelligence. I don't want some overeducated pedantic type with no practical experience. I want someone who has experience with the topic and who is really willing to talk candidly.

A good example of what I am talking about is former LAPD detective Mark Fuhrman, who I often have on my show talking about criminal cases. Fuhrman, you may recall, was the detective in the O.J. Simpson case who was caught using the word *nigger* years earlier and who the defense team accused of planting evidence. Fuhrman became synonymous with the word *racist*.

Now, many viewers have gotten mad at me for using Fuhrman as often as I have on my show. Here is some of what they and I have said to each other:

To: ontherecord@foxnews.com
From: Carolyn in Fairmont, West Virginia

From 8 P.M. to 11 P.M. every night my television is tuned to Fox News. I am a huge fan (O'Reilly is my favorite), so I feel I can offer some constructive criticism. Frankly, it disgusts me to see Fox use the likes of Mark Fuhrman as a "Fox News contributor." This man is a racist rogue cop who committed perjury in a murder trial and may have directly affected the outcome of that case with his criminal actions. He too should have been prosecuted. Therefore, I feel he does not deserve to be showcased as an expert detective.

Carolyn—thanks for writing. Let me tell you my view of Mark Fuhrman. For many years I did criminal defense work and represented minorities and saw firsthand the terrible way the system treated them and continues to do so. Having said that, Mark Fuhrman did wrong and was punished. I think, like all who have done wrong and paid the penalty, we should be willing to let the person back into our good graces. This does not mean I agree with his behavior but rather that since he paid the price I can forgive.

I appreciate these viewers' concerns, but I will continue to book Mark Fuhrman, and I stand behind my years of work doing civil rights litigation and representing minorities. And I stand behind Mark Fuhrman as a guest because he is a good detective. As a criminal defense lawyer, I dealt with a lot of detectives. Mark Fuhrman is one of the smartest and best detectives I have ever come across. He does not just show up on TV and yak about the case. He has done his homework and actually thought through the case we are discussing. I appreciate how thorough he is and how he really examines whatever evidence is available to the public.

Yes, Mark Fuhrman did wrong. He was wrong to use the racial slur, and he was wrong to deny it under oath. The first was immoral and the second illegal. But Mark paid his dues. He pleaded guilty and he successfully completed his probation. I believe that we all need to let someone back into the community when he has paid the price. I believe in rehabilitation. And I believe he deserves another chance. If he fails again, I don't think I will be forgiving.

GUESTS FROM HELL AND THE ORGANIZATION MAN . . . OR WOMAN

Guests from hell come in many shapes. I religiously police the show's selection of guests every day, but sometimes one will slip by who is (there no way to be diplomatic here) a nightmare.

Nothing infuriates me more than when I get someone who has an agenda and who appears to answer questions from an invisible script. You've seen those guests. You know what I mean. They don't answer the question directly but launch into a two-minute speech.

For instance:

Greta: Is the president's economic stimulus package really going to help the economy?

Guest: Thank you, Greta, for inviting me here, and before I get to that, I want to commend the president for his strong stand on abortion. Our country . . .

If you watch my shows over the years, you will see that I rarely have a guest who is a spokesperson from an organization. My producers are familiar with my rallying cry: "No groups! I hate groups!" It's not that organizations are inherently bad or that I don't agree with any of them. But many times the representatives are simply employees. They promote the group's agenda rather than expressing strong personal convictions. It makes me feel like I'm part of a propaganda operation. You've heard the names of these organizations: People for the American Way (does that mean I am against the American way if I don't agree?) or Concerned Women for America (so I am not a concerned woman of America if I don't agree?).

And then there's the guest who has neither an agenda nor personal convictions, someone who agrees with me on everything. I don't want that either. Besides the challenge of debating someone with a different view of an issue, for selfish reasons I want to book guests who don't agree with me. Remember, I don't want to be bored either!

Believe it or not, there is an art to booking the debate guest. Besides wanting to book someone who is lively and passionate—a wishy-washy person is fatal to TV—my first choice is to book someone who disagrees with me. I can agree with myself—that's neither a challenge nor fun! Debating on television is like tennis: You want to debate someone who just may be smarter and more experienced than you are. It ups your game. While it's fun to win a debate, the truth is that it is more fun to be challenged. I deliberately try to get guests who are great news tennis players.

There is nothing worse than the "yup" guest. The dialogue goes like this:

Greta: So, we should go to war now and not wait for the United Nations to pass a resolution.

Guest: Yup.

Greta: You agree?

Guest: Yup.

Greta: And weather could be a real problem if we wait.

Guest: Yup.

Greta: But we need to take the capital city slowly, so as to minimize the casualties. Moving too quickly could cause terrorists to unleash chemical weapons. Do you think that's true?

Guest: Yup.

Just when I am ready to shoot myself at a moment like this, the producer is saying in my ear, "Six minutes." Do you know what six minutes is in television? It's more than a lifetime. In television, six minutes with a bad guest is eternity. It means you now have to think of some way to get your guest to talk, debate, any-thing—just stop saying "yup."

I much prefer this any day:

Greta: We should go to war now and not wait for the United Nations.

Guest: You are wrong. If we don't get the support from the global community, we are going to start World War III. It will enrage the entire Arab community and give North Korea a chance to act up while our attention is diverted.

Now, having brilliantly set forth my foolproof formula for great guests, I confess it has not always been a smooth ride. I still get my share. Take, for instance, what might be called the inter-view from hell. This was on October 24, 2002, during the sniper scare in Washington, D.C., and shortly after John Allen Muham-mad was named as the key suspect in the shootings.

Greta: Joining me from Tacoma, Washington, is Carl Jones. He lives on the same street at John Allen Muhammad. Thank you for joining us tonight. Carl.

Carl Jones: Thank you.

Greta: Carl, when did you first hear of or meet Mr. John Muhammad?

Jones: I have never met him.

Greta: But you lived on the same street, right?

Jones: I live one street over.

Greta: Did you ever become aware of him or know of him?

Jones: Oh, I've seen him in the neighborhood.

Greta: And under what circumstances?

Jones: Just going around in the neighborhood.

Greta: And when was that?

Jones: Probably about a year ago.

Greta: Did he ever do anything unusual?

Jones: Not that I seen.

Greta: Did you ever—was he a good neighbor?

Jones: I didn't know him.

Greta: Did you ever hear gunshots?

Jones: Yes. About a little more than a year ago, I heard three rapid shots and called the police.

Greta: And did you know from what neighbor, from what house you heard the gunshots?

Jones: Oh, close. Very close.

Greta: And did you identify John Muhammad's house as the address from which you heard the sounds of gunshots?

Jones: I had no idea where they came from.

Greta: Do you know if the police ever responded to the scene and investigated your complaint?

Jones: I hope so, but I didn't go out to look.

Greta: Did you ever ask or find out?

Jones: No, I didn't.

Greta: Did any other neighbors ever make any remarks to you about John Muhammad or any noise of gunshots from his house?

Jones: No.

Greta: All right, Carl, thank you very much for joining us.

As I stumbled through this horrible experience, I kept thinking, *Why is he here? Why am I talking to this man?* I kept thinking that maybe it wasn't as bad as I felt it was, maybe the viewers wouldn't notice—maybe it just felt worse to me.

No such luck. The interview came across as bad as it felt. Viewers wrote chastising me and telling me that I never should have booked him.

To: ontherecord@foxnews.com
From: Brian in Acton, Massachussetts

I'm so sorry, Greta! Greta, I love your show, and watch it as much as I can. But holy cow . . . does your show have a producer? How could they let you hang out to dry with that "neighbor" of John Allen Muhammad, who lived one street over, never met the suspect, and never talked to the suspect? I thought you handled the situation as best as you could with your questions, but it was clear your piece wasn't going anywhere. What's your producer's e-mail? I would love to tell them what I think! Keep up the great work, Greta.

Brian—I think that interview was the worst moment in television . . . ugh.

To: ontherecord@foxnews.com
From: Tom in Greeneville, Tennessee

Greta: Good interview of Muhammad's neighbor. Many more like that and your rating will be number .1.

My thoughts to viewers: Do you really think I booked him? Would I really do that to the audience, much less to myself? Do I appear to be that much of a masochist?

FALSE EXPERTS ARE DEAD WEIGHT TOO, AND THE VIEWERS CAN SMELL IT

Sometimes the worst of times coincides with the best of times. Despite that disaster with the unknown neighbor, *On the Record* covered the sniper investigation quite thoroughly, and we did something I'm proud of, something different from what many of the other news shows did: We deliberately did not book criminal profilers.

Profilers are supposed to be experts in predicting what kind of person—character, nature, and habits—is likely to be responsible for a certain kind of crime. Profilers engage in the type of discussion I love to have around a dinner table with friends and family. It's fun to guess and theorize—but that's all it is. It's not scientific. And it's fraud to try to pass it off to viewers as a valid method for investigating a crime.

In all my years of doing criminal work, I cannot recall a

profiler solving a single crime. Not once. My experience is that all crimes are solved the old-fashioned way—good detective work and tips.

People get tired of me saying it's always clues and tips, clues and tips, but it's true. I want to book detectives and people intimately involved in criminal investigations. Profilers provide interesting chatter, but ultimately they give an unrealistic presentation to the viewers.

If you disagree with me, I invite you to prove me wrong about profilers. Give me one example where profiling has caught a suspect. Sometimes profiling can be useful, interesting, or even (rarely) accurate. But profilers' theories almost never result in an arrest.

All the profilers in the sniper investigation said the shooter was a white man and a loner. It turned out to be two black men.

I can give you lots of other examples of when profilers have failed us. In the Polly Klaas murder case, for instance, profilers pointed to someone who knew the little girl. They said it was unlikely a complete stranger would crawl in through a bedroom window and kidnap a little girl. They were wrong: Richard Allen Davis picked the house in Petaluma, California, at random.

Another good example is Ted Kaczynski. For years Kaczynski, the Unabomber, was profiled and profiled as the FBI tried to find out who was sending mail bombs to academics and businesses around the country. Profilers said he was a loner who was intelligent. Duh! Anybody could tell that by reading his writings! But in the end he was caught because his brother turned him in after his writings were published in two newspapers. This is the old-fashioned way—clues and tips. The evidence came in the form of a clue (the writings) and a tip (his brother's call after recognizing the writings). Nothing the profilers said led to his arrest.

The ratings of our show during the sniper investigation were high, including one night when they were the highest on all of cable television. I believe that was because smart viewers knew our guests were people who were either part of the story or had hands-on experience and stuck to the facts. Viewers are seldom fooled, and their attention is often a good indicator of superfluous hype, false experts, or the same old same old.

It only takes a second before the viewers' attention wanders and their thumbs start working the remote. I might lose them to sleep, or to pizza, or to another network. But you know I'll discover it at my desk tomorrow afternoon, and you can bet I will try to fix it. News is important and does not have to be dull. I owe it to my viewers not to be boring.

2

NEW PATRIOTISM
AND THE MILITARY

Liberty isn't free. As a nation, we must provide for the men and women who put their lives on the line for us. That means good pay, adequate funding for defense, and our heartfelt support. Vietnam was a very long time ago. We baby boomers have to wake up and realize that today's military is different from the one we grew up with, and we are fighting a very different war. Patriotism is not a conservative or liberal thing. Patriotism, as far as I am concerned, is the duty and obligation of every American.

Do you remember when you were a kid in elementary school and you first learned about Paul Revere's midnight ride? Couldn't you practically hear the sound of horse hooves on the cobblestone streets of Boston? The stories of our nation's beginnings quickened your heart with urgency and bravery. It's patriotism, and even a child understands what it's made of. These guys—George Washington, Thomas Jefferson, Patrick Henry— would die for their liberty, our freedom. It was thrilling then, and it's thrilling still. I grew up in an era that initially was defined by the very real and very chilling backdrop of the Cold War. The Soviet Union was a serious and dangerous enemy. Our school and most public buildings had fallout shelters, places stockpiled with canned foods and identifiable by black-and-yellow signs. The real power of a nuclear bomb was fresh in people's minds.

I remember vividly the Memorial Day parades of my childhood, where the heroes of World War I and World War II were showcased through the streets of my hometown. I was too young to understand what these men had done or why my parents and everyone else in town considered them heroes, but the pomp and the music were stirring, and I couldn't take my eyes off those military dress uniforms. Little did I realize that my generation was on the brink of something that would change us all, forever.

THE VIETNAM WAR AND PATRIOTISM

By the time I was a teenager, the public eye focused on a whole new image of war, and the public conversation was filled with words no one had heard before: *napalm, guerilla, demilitarized zone.*

Gone were the war movies of an earlier generation, the kind like *To Hell and Back* or *Sands of Iwo Jima.* The glory of those Veterans of Foreign Wars parades vanished in our culture. My generation got movies like *Full Metal Jacket* and *Platoon.* We would hear that Marines raped Vietnamese women and smoked marijuana.

TV shows like *M*A*S*H*—which of course was set in Korea, but was intended to reflect the realities of Vietnam—captured the cynicism of this latest military effort—a sentiment very different from the valiant one with which my parents' generation fought their war. Television airtime was filled with footage of choppers and napalmed civilians, of protesting college kids at Kent State University in Ohio (midwestern kids like me) gunned down by the National Guard.

I particularly remember hearing about the killing of more than five hundred Vietnamese civilians by U.S. soldiers in a small village called My Lai on March 16, 1968. When news of this event was reported a year or so later, and after the court-martial of Lieutenant William Calley, under whose command the massacre and rapes and torture had occurred . . . well, this was a very different view of our military. What happened to the soldier hero, the American icon?

Our country suffered with this war in a way that was completely different from what we had experienced in previous wars. It tore us apart. There were no Audie Murphys of my generation, no Churchills, no Eisenhowers. What we took away from the Vietnam War was skepticism of our military. Our disapproval of the Vietnam War translated into disapproval of the military. And the word *patriotic* stuck in our throats.

I have learned a lot since then. All I heard about back in the 1960s and 1970s were men like Lieutenant Calley. I didn't hear about men like Hugh Thompson Johnson, and I wish I had.

On that infamous afternoon on March 16, 1968, the day of the My Lai massacre, Hugh Thompson, a warrant officer in the army, was flying his Scout helicopter over My Lai when he saw army officers gunning down civilians lying in a ditch.

"I saw Americans approaching an opening to a bunker where I could see an old man, an old woman, and a little baby," Thompson said. "I realized they had about fifteen seconds to live."

Thompson swooped his helicopter down between the civilians and the troops. With his crew chief and gunner covering him, he ordered the U.S. soldiers to stop firing and threatened to open fire on them if they continued.

They stopped. Some 504 villagers lay dead, but Thompson's amazing actions are credited with saving the rest of the villagers.

Like every other vet from the Vietnam era, Thompson received no hero's welcome for his actions when he came home to Louisiana, and instead some in the army threatened him. It took some thirty years for Thompson and his two men, Lawrence Colburn and Glenn Andreotta (who was killed three weeks after the incident), to gain recognition. They were awarded the Soldier's Medal, the highest award for bravery not involving conflict with the enemy.

Thompson insists he was not a hero, that he was just doing the right thing. In my view, he did do the right thing, but he is also a hero.

I wish as a teenager I had heard about Hugh Thompson, whom I interviewed on my CNN show once, long ago. Because I know in my heart that it is the Hugh Thompsons who represent the real men and women in our armed forces, not the William Calleys. What a shame so many people remember Calley's name but not Hugh Thompson's.

I believe that the good men and women who answered the call back then, who answered the draft in the face of a very unpopular war, and who never had parades on their return, should be saluted today. I was formed by the stories of our country's beginnings: stories about bravery and standing up for what's right. Maybe that, and my father's example, drew me toward the law. Even now, as a talking head on cable news, I feel it's my civic duty to host public debate, to practice our liberty of discourse. In some quarters, a patriot is anybody who agrees with your own viewpoint. That is wrong. We should be wise and cautious when we question someone's patriotism. Disagreeing or having a different point of view does not mean you are a traitor. You can have a different idea and still be a patriot.

When it comes to patriotism, here's the real question: Would I lay down my life for the values we cherish most? Would you?

Could we utter and mean the words that the thirty-eight-year-old self-taught lawyer Patrick Henry did on that extraordinary day on March 23, 1775, before the delegates in Virginia: "What would they have? Is life so dear, or peace so sweet, as to be purchased at the price of chains and slavery? Forbid it, Almighty God! I know not what course others may take, but as for me, give me liberty or give me death!"

Soldiers on the front lines are in essence saying those words every day. The fact is, not enough of us value the sacrifice members of the military make for us each day. And now, especially after September 11, 2001, and the war in Iraq, it's time we looked at the hard reality of what our world is like today. A strong military is necessary, and so is our strong support of it!

The first time, post-Vietnam, that the reality of military service hit me was when I was twenty-six years old and went to Normandy, France. I had recently graduated from law school. I remember looking up at those vertical cliffs and I tried to imagine our soldiers in World War II scaling them. I couldn't do it if I had the entire day and no one was shooting at me.

Afterward I went to one of the cemeteries at Normandy. There are fifteen thousand white markers there, and it is terribly quiet. Besides the grief from the loss, you cannot help but feel awe for their bravery.

THE GOOD SHIP

Recently I did something I never imagined I'd do. I boarded a small military airplane in Norfolk, Virginia, and tail-hooked onto a vessel in the Atlantic. And what a vessel it is! The magnificent USS *Harry S Truman*, one of the colossal nuclear aircraft carriers, one very flashy example of our military might.

This thing, this floating airstrip I flew into, is as long as the Empire State Building is tall and has four and a half acres of flight deck. It is *big*. And to give you an idea of what kind of a floating metropolis it is, it serves up 18,150 meals a day, has 2,000 telephones onboard, and has 2,700 compartments. Plus it can go 30 knots (about 30 mph), quite fast for a ship.

Upon hitting the deck, what stopped us short and kept our plane from skidding into the Atlantic was the tail hook, a hook bolted to an eight-foot bar extending from the aft part of the aircraft. It is with the tail hook that the pilot catches one of four steel cables stretched across the deck, bringing our plane, traveling at 150 miles per hour, to a complete stop in about 320 feet. You do the math . . . that's sudden. The cables are set to stop each aircraft at the same place on the deck, regardless of the size or weight of the plane.

We hit the deck, the tail hook grabbed the line, and we were abruptly stopped. I cannot describe the exhilaration. I was amazed. I stepped out, looked around, and let my imagination soar; I was eighteen again and choosing my future.

Given the choice, would I choose law school? Or would I think about the military, consider serving my country aboard a carrier this magnificent?

Even considering such a thing was a collision with all the nightmarish things I had thought about the military, growing up in the Vietnam era. But this was a different world, a different time, and you could absolutely feel it in your bones standing on that flight deck. These young men and women had honor, courage, principles, no skepticism, and plenty of blue sky. I did feel envy—I wish I had their sense of duty and honor.

WHAT IT TAKES TO UNRATTLE MY CAGE: BIG JETS AND TRUSTWORTHY YOUNG WARRIORS

Let me tell you another story: I try to visit as many military bases as possible on my show so that viewers can really see what our armed services are doing. I loved going to Fort Leonard, an army base in Missouri, and crawling inside a German-designed vehicle that tests for chemical and biological weapons. They call it "the Fox," which I especially liked!

But on another occasion I was picked up at the gate of Whiteman Air Force Base in Warrensburg, Missouri, about 60 miles southeast of Kansas City. The landscape around the base was familiar to me, green and moist and solidly midwestern. The public information officer had driven me over rolling farmlands and past sandstone quarries into a vast concrete compound secured with electric fencing and razor wire.

The secure area looked like something out of a science fiction movie. Cameras were everywhere for security, and colossal hangars for the thing I'd come to see: an enormous and invisible plane.

We turned the corner, and my eye caught sight of her—the B-2 Stealth bomber. This was a giant metal entity, half manta ray, half spaceship *Enterprise*. She was sitting there looking both majestic and threatening. She was bad, and I loved her.

I met several pilots of the B-2—the crème de la crème of our air force. Like the navy sailors, they exuded confidence and good humor. In spite of the scares that have rippled through our nation since September 11, 2001, these men and women made me feel safe. In the news business we deal with scares 24/7, but I feel the same as you every time a yellow alert gets elevated to an orange alert: What should I be doing, not as a news anchor but as a citizen? Should I be scared? Where do I run?

So it was reassuring to spend time with these folks. Let's put it this way: My cage got unrattled for the time being. I could forget smallpox, anthrax, ricin, dirty bombs, the lot.

The air force has twenty-one B-2 Stealth bombers. Sixteen can do the work of a thousand fighter planes. They fly slowly, but radar can't find them. They deliver bombs with IQs, meaning we can tell the bombs what to hit and the bombs obey.

In climbing into the cockpit, I was surprised at how small it is. I could not imagine sitting in such a small place for sixteen hours straight. But the pilot I interviewed made it seem so exciting that I again was jealous. Maybe sixteen hours seemed like ten seconds. I confess I think I could do without the midair refueling—that's when another aircraft lingers just a few feet above the B-2 while refueling. I cannot imagine what that must be like.

In thinking back, the reason I was so awed by the air force, army, and navy is that the members of the military are proud and have honor. They are devoid of cynicism and hold the principles of country close to their hearts.

PAYCHECKS AND PAYLOADS

So today I find myself wondering: Are we compensating our soldiers fairly? It is indeed hard to understand how in the year 2002, the U.S. Congress voted the military only a 4.1% raise. I can't figure out why the public servants who risk their lives should get an insignificant raise. This embarrasses me.

But perhaps more importantly, are we giving our military what it needs? It really does not make sense to cut corners when the world is this dangerous and the risks are life-threatening to them (and also to us). This is not to say we should be buying the $600 toilet seat that the Pentagon became famous for years ago. But here's what it does mean. We need to upgrade old aircraft and weapons. Defense secretary Donald Rumsfeld has pushed a plan to upgrade space-based communications, including navigation and early-warning satellites, and he is right. One of the Lacrosse imaging satellites—those are the ones that can see through clouds and in the dark—flying over Iraq is more than ten years old. Three of the other five imaging satellites over Iraq were launched in the mid-1990s. These satellites need to be upgraded to make the best use of their capacities. We need to fund aircraft like the EA-6B Prowler, which uses bursts of electromagnetic energy to disarm enemy radar and wireless communications.

I am not, in the general sense and without addressing any particular conflict, a person who supports war. Who does? But if we need to go to war, let's be smart. And what could be smarter than developing technology that saves us from having to use bombs at all?

THE DRAFT

Debate has begun in some circles—and is sure to continue—as to whether our nation should return to the draft. The argument in favor is that it is "fair"—that it would require everyone of age to serve, not just some, and so will democratize the force. That's a phony argument. The draft was never fair. When I was growing up, if you were from an upper-middle-class family, the draft meant one of the following: You went to school and got a deferment, or you ended up in the National Guard. And let's face it, there was a big difference between the National Guard and Saigon.

The draft also did nothing for the morale of the military. I can't think of an institution where morale is so important as for our military. If you had to be drafted, you didn't want to be there. And if you are threatened with the coercion of the draft, as my generation was during the Vietnam War, something else can happen. It's not that you become antiwar, which is one thing; you also can become antimilitary, which is entirely different.

I believe in the right to be antiwar, but I think being antimilitary undermines our country.

My impression of our military today—and admittedly, my contact has been minimal, and I was shown the crown jewels—is that morale is good despite our nation's unwillingness to compensate the men and women serving in uniform in a fashion I believe to be appropriate and fair. Perhaps that says even more about the men and women in uniform—that despite the less-than-fair compensation, they serve us with great skill and great zeal.

Frankly (and maybe this seems a bit kooky), as we face the military challenges ahead, I would not be opposed to some voluntary civilian service, which would allow those of us who are a bit older to help in the military effort. Certainly there is something I could do to help on a few weekends a year.

As this book went to press America was close to victory in the war with Iraq. Almost immediately, it seemed, those who supported the war started poking nasty jabs at those who were opposed to it. I think that is a mistake. We need to look forward and not back, except to use history to teach us and guide us about the future. Looking back to find blame and point fingers is stupid. Remember, what ultimately separates us from Saddam and his regime is that we *can* disagree. In pre-Saddam days, when you disagreed, you were "lucky" simply to have your tongue cut out. Many people were summarily executed for speaking their mind. I love America. We have free speech and a right to debate. We need to foster that debate and praise it, not stifle it. In the end, debate and disagreement are very good things. They make us think, which then leads to the exercise of good judgment.

And, as we declare victory, we need to remind ourselves that the problem in Iraq was not ended just because the gunfire stopped. Huge humanitarian issues must be confronted. I hope the news agencies show as much enthusiasm for these issues as they did in the fighting. How about "embedding" journalists among the suffering Iraqi civilians so we can get the best information we can?

3

THE DEATH PENALTY

The death penalty should be legal and available to courts and juries . . . but it should be used extremely rarely, and only when we are absolutely certain that a fair trial has taken place.

D O YOU EVER TURN ON YOUR TELEVISION and wonder if those folks yakking away have any idea what they're talking about? I do. Worse, I watch lawyers on TV spouting opinions about trial strategy and I know they have never been inside a courtroom! How can you talk about trials from an "expert" position if you've never even tried a case? Well, I like to apply that same standard to my own opinion spouting. I may not always succeed, but I promise that I try my damnedest. And the fact is that I often talked about the death penalty when I first became a legal analyst on television.

Right from the beginning of O.J. Simpson's criminal trial, there was talk of the death penalty. Remember? It was a big deal when the Los Angeles district attorney was deciding whether or not to ask for the death penalty for Simpson. Everybody knew that might have an effect on the jury—if the DA asked for the death penalty, the jurors would be burdened by the knowledge that they could be sending an American football hero to his death instead of considering whether in fact he was guilty of murder. In such a case, where the possibility of execution is going to distract jurors, prosecutors often elect not to seek the death penalty, which is what they did in the Simpson trial.

Now, I know more about the death penalty than the average person. For fifteen years before I started my television career I was a real lawyer practicing criminal defense. During that time my criminal defense firm had several clients who faced execution. I think nearly every criminal defense attorney is against the death penalty. There's too great a margin of error to risk the ultimate punishment. The deck is stacked against poorer defendants. I think the O.J. Simpson case poisoned the American people's view of what criminal trials really are, but it was such an aberration. No wonder people are so quick to say "Off with his head!" as soon as someone is convicted.

The fact is that the routine murder trial is deplorable. Murder trials in Texas, for example, can take as little as three days! I can't begin to describe some of the sad-sack, grossly incompetent lawyers who are appointed to represent impoverished defendants and have even—this is true!—fallen asleep during trial. Public defenders don't have the funds for discovery, DNA testing, or even the testing of hair and fiber evidence. Innocent people do get convicted! Based on DNA evidence, some 123 convicted people who were on death row have been exonerated by the efforts of Barry Scheck's Innocence Project. As far as I am concerned, that is way too many mistakes! In fact, I believe that one mistake in a death penalty case is one mistake too many.

Go to Mississippi, go to Texas, and take a look at how those trials are conducted. The law demands and promises fairness, but frequently—as we've come to see again and again with DNA evidence—we *don't* deliver a fair verdict, and innocent people are put to death. That's how a criminal defense lawyer looks at it. That's how I looked at it too. In the early '90s I stopped being a practicing attorney with a constitutionally mandated responsibility to give even the most heinous client the best representation possible, and I became a legal analyst for a national television network. And when you work in journalism you are forced to see grays instead of black and white. Your job ceases to be that of the pure advocate and becomes instead the voice of balance and fairness. To reflect reality and find the truth, you have to look at all sides. The death penalty is the great crucible issue in America these days, particularly after the terrorist acts of September 11, 2001. There is no issue more divisive, more heated, more emotional, or more complex, other than perhaps abortion. And it's only become more serious over the past decade. Between 1977 and 1982 only six people were executed in the United States. The pace picked up slightly after that: Eleven people were executed in 1988, and fourteen in 1991. But hold on. In 1997, seventy-four people were executed in America. That, however, was nothing compared to 1999, when ninety-eight people were put to death. That pace has slowed a bit—there were seventy-one executions in 2002, and thirty-three of those were in Texas.

Anyway, back to my own matter of trying to know what I am talking about on television. Not long ago I realized that despite all those years as a defense lawyer fighting for the life of my own clients, I had never seen anybody executed. I didn't know what it was like. Eating popcorn while watching a video of *Dead Man Walking* just doesn't count. I didn't really know what was involved, and I often worried that it made me a fraud when discussing executions. Be careful what you wish for. One day, not long after covering the Timothy McVeigh trial and more than a year before he was executed, I got the so-called opportunity to witness an execution in Virginia. I thought about all those years my law firm had spent trying to save clients from the chair. After thinking about McVeigh, I thought, *Okay, step up to the plate. Go see what you are really talking about here.*

We arrived at the prison very late in the evening. We could feel the tension in the dark air. It was eerie in the prison yard and inside the prison. You could feel the execution in the air. The warden told me that the other inmates all knew that a man was about to die. Everyone was on edge.

Soon I was introduced to the team who would execute the prisoner. The entire execution team seemed like the kind of people who could be your neighbor. They wore a sort of uniform, but they still looked like the postman or the school crossing guard. And then it hit me: Each *was* someone's neighbor. Each was just a regular person with a really weird job.

The team kept repeating the word *professional,* and I politely nodded as each explained to me what exactly he did during the execution. It was done almost as a way of detaching themselves from the task. "We do things professionally here," said one man, almost as though there were executions elsewhere that weren't professional. Was this a way to convince ourselves that we weren't in the Middle East stoning someone? Anyway, each time they said that I realized how bizarre this experience was. Here I was, in a maximum-security prison, standing in the execution area's viewing room with these extremely nice people who were very proud of their work—and their work was killing people. Ever go into an electronics store and an enthusiastic salesman shows you the latest DVD player, then demonstrates it with pride? It was kind of like that—just people who were proud of their work and eager to talk about it with a group of strangers.

Before the execution they served the eighteen or so media people sandwiches and potato chips. Then there was what felt like a mad dash for the "best seats" in the front row. We were seated in a glass-enclosed room with an unobstructed view of the death chamber. Already feeling queasy, I chose a seat toward the rear. The execution chamber filled up with the execution team and some suits, administrative types in the Virginia prison system. From where I sat I couldn't hear them, but they all stood around talking as though they were gathered to meet about changing the prison menu.

Suddenly a door to the side swung open forcefully and the condemned man was swept through, with corrections officers holding him on each side. With what seemed like a single gesture, they swiftly placed him on the gurney and belted him down. If I had blinked, I would have missed it all. They swabbed the prisoner's arm with an alcohol-soaked cotton ball at the spot where the lethal needle was to be placed. (Later I asked someone why the disinfectant, and I couldn't believe the answer: so there would be no infection. No infection? You are about to kill the guy and you're worried about infection? Talk about bureaucracy.)

The signal was given, and the execution began. The warden read something to the prisoner (presumably the death warrant), then paused and looked at the phone on the wall, which was a direct line to the governor's office. It didn't ring. There would be no eleventh-hour reprieve. The warden nodded slowly to the executioner. The man on the gurney lifted his head and looked straight at us in the media room. He screamed out something like, "God, I am sorry!" He set his head down, shivered, and died. The curtain was drawn. It was over. I felt dirty. I wanted out. Fast.

I have always been against the death penalty. There's the law, and there's the two sides of the argument, one argued by the prosecution and the other by the defense. Of course the law itself varies from state to state. Each has a formula for which crimes warrant the death penalty, but essentially it comes down to aggravating circumstances, such as the severity or cruelty of the crime, and mitigating factors, such as the fact that the criminal went to church and had no criminal history. In any case, the prosecution argues that the law says execution is allowed, the jury convicted the defendant, and he should have thought more before he committed this crime. It is essentially an eye-for-an-eye argument. The defense argues that the jury probably made a mistake in convicting his client, and that even if they didn't and he is guilty, his life is worth saving.

Like I said, I think nearly every criminal defense lawyer is against the death penalty. Of course, I'm not against justice in the form of fair punishment; give somebody a fair trial and let the jury system work. If somebody is found guilty of a crime such as murder, put him away for life, no parole. But killing a human being, no matter how bad he is, seems to me to make the system nearly as bad as the criminal. Or at least that's what I thought I believed.

Then I covered the Timothy McVeigh trial. I always thought that during my career as a lawyer trying cases I had seen everything: photos of burned bodies, autopsy photos, photos of tortured people, photos of bodies undiscovered for days after death. I thought I had developed a pretty strong stomach for the business. I had a rude awakening with the McVeigh trial. The number of deaths (168), the photos of the children who died, and the injured victims who had trekked to Denver to watch the trial had a painful impact on me. Seeing victims with missing limbs passing me in the hallway outside the courtroom was sometimes more difficult than seeing the photos of the dead. I looked at these people, burned and battered, and realized that one day they'd woken up, gone to work, and had their lives changed forever. I would imagine how their breakfast that day had seemed so normal, so usual. And they'd had no idea that within an hour or so, their lives would never be the same. Some would be blinded. Others would not walk again. I had never seen devastation and suffering like that before.

I was stunned by the sheer scope of it—imagining the cries of fifteen-year-old Brandy Liggons, who had been trapped twelve hours in a web of twisted metal and electrical conduits by the time rescuers reached her, or the sight of three hundred families coming to the local church carrying photos and dental records of their children and their wives to help identify their bodies and yet hoping they'd somehow be found alive. After that trial I thought I might change my views on the death penalty after all. If anybody deserved to die, it was McVeigh. Yet watching that execution in Virginia confused me all over again.

So how do I feel now about the death penalty? Well, I have to say that September 11 altered my views again. My conclusion may not please everyone, and it may seem to be a cop-out in this time of "You're either with us or against us!" But hard-line thinking on this issue is impossible—that is what I've concluded after the past several years of covering terrorist events. Each case is so different. An absolute position for all cases is not the position that a thinking person will take on this issue. But what I know to be true is this: There is more to the death penalty than "Did he or didn't he?" and "Should we or shouldn't we?" Like an atom, it is composed of many particles. It is this nutty which-side-are-you-on mentality that has poisoned all careful thinking and in some instances fostered a trigger-happy mentality from both hardcore advocates who argue and protest for it as well as from those opposed to the death penalty who wouldn't admit a murder happened even if it occurred before their eyes. Zealots on either side of this issue—as with any important issue—are dangerous.

I believe there are instances when the death penalty is appropriate. But there are instances where it is not. Here is where it is not appropriate: We cannot kill innocent people, and we absolutely must recognize that we have done so in the past. And unless we guarantee that trials will be fair—meaning with competent legal counsel and adequate resources for defense—we are going to execute innocent people. We also cannot kill legally insane people. And we can never kill minors, period.

Who wants to execute an innocent person? No one. Yet we have an enormous willingness to conduct half-baked trials and provide the poor with incompetent lawyers or underfunded public defenders who don't have the resources to properly investigate crimes and conduct discovery. In those cases we run a high risk of executing the innocent.

For horrible crimes such as the bombing of the Murrah Building in Oklahoma, we had some whiners who thought that Timothy McVeigh should live. But he was a cold-blooded killer. Tell me one reason why he should live after doing what he did and after enjoying a $12 million defense. He got a fair trial.

Timothy McVeigh got the death penalty the old-fashioned way: He earned it. The cases where a criminal defendant had a fair defense and a real trial are all too rare. High-profile trials like McVeigh's and O.J. Simpson's are an aberration. We can't pretend otherwise.

But here is where the death penalty is appropriate: In the case of a truly heinous crime where there is a fair trial, such as McVeigh's, I have no objection to the death penalty. And what about the terrorists who killed three thousand people on September 11? Some people have been shocked when I say that I think lethal injection is too humane for them. I know it is an emotional response, but terrorists who claim credit for killing innocent people should be executed after a fair trial. We are living in a new world after September 11, with crimes that we couldn't imagine a decade ago.

For me, it always comes down to this: fair trials and a sound justice system. I do not oppose the death penalty as long as there is a fair trial and competent counsel. Is that the position I would have taken ten years ago as a defense attorney? No, it is not. But back then I had a job that was mandated by the U.S. Constitution. My job was to provide the best legal counsel possible to defend my client, no matter what the crime or the guilt.

But times change, opinions change. My job back then was different, and I had a duty as a lawyer. I will never change my position that the Constitution demands a fair justice system, and I do not think the death penalty can be taken lightly or prescribed as carelessly as it is in America today. The death penalty should be a deterrent, and if it is commonplace, if we can't even remember the name of the last person executed in this country, we will forget just how serious it is.

Justice is expensive, but in the end it is what sets us apart from other nations. We don't take shortcuts in this democracy, and we pride ourselves on fairness.

Of course, I have my private and personal thoughts and feelings about heinous killers—those who have committed cold-hearted, premeditated murders, terrorists who have tried to destroy our country. I am angry, and I want to get them! But I want to know that my nation did it the right way, upholding the standards and principles that make us the greatest country. We can convict people fair and square. And when we do, we refuse to stoop to the level of those who would threaten and hurt us.

4

ON LOYALTY
AND CONFLICT

People who like each other—even love each other—can disagree. They can fight. What is better than spirited debate? But it doesn't need to get personal, and it should never become mean. Also, mistakes happen; it's people who make them. It's critical to admit your mistakes, pay the piper, and move on. As for the rest of you—get over it!

I DON'T THINK THERE ARE MANY SUBJECTS AS DEAR to my heart as the topic of a good fight. Come on, I'm a lawyer—I'm paid to argue. But for me the ability to disagree with people and maintain respect and affection is a fundamental value. I believe in good strong aggressive debate.

The writer Annie Lamott wondered aloud if people who are cruel get sent to the mean-people's room in heaven. I wonder too. Why do we have to be mean and call each other names when we disagree about something, whether it is abortion, the death penalty, tax policy, or homeland security? Why the finger-pointing and the challenging of other people's patriotism? Why has good old-fashioned disagreement suddenly turned into a question about moral character and patriotism?

I don't think we have to be cruel and personal. I'm not naive, and I am not the sweetest person in the world. But I think the level of rancor we see in politics today cheapens the quality of our national debate. And it is exactly this quality—we Americans can disagree and fight with each other, hold fierce electoral campaigns, and yet not shoot and kill each other—that distinguishes our two-hundred-year history of democracy from the rest of the world. That's not the way it is in Iran or North Korea. If we do not protect that open quality of our public life, we are finished.

Let's start with a major national nonissue: my arrival at Fox News. A lot of people flew out of their skins when Fox hired me. Wasn't I a liberal Democrat over at CNN? Hadn't I defended Bill Clinton and O.J. Simpson? How could I possibly go to Fox, the conservative cable network? Leaving CNN was one thing, Greta, but going to Fox?

Everybody went nuts. The conservatives hated me before they even knew me, and the liberals felt betrayed. Even people who had never seen me on television seemed to have an opinion.

Now wait a minute. Let's put aside the fact that nobody really knew my personal opinions on anything. I had never taken any big public political positions, so how did people form these ideas? And who says I have to agree with everyone I work with or they have to agree with me? I didn't agree with everything said at CNN. I don't agree with everything said at Fox. I don't agree with everything my husband thinks either, but I still love him.

What I need to worry about is what *I* think, not what somebody else thinks. What I say on my show are my words, my thoughts, my opinions, and my ideas. Frankly, from time to time, as I rethink matters and as the facts change, my ideas and opinions change. Nobody tells me what to say; nobody tells me what my views are. They didn't do it at CNN when I was there, and they haven't done it at Fox.

When I first met Roger Ailes, the head of Fox News Channel, I wanted to see if he was serious about being "fair and balanced," which is the famous Fox motto. We talked for many hours, and I got it that Roger meant what he said. We all have our personal political views—anybody who says journalists and broadcasters don't have views is just plain lying—but the key issue is what you put on the air.

People have opinions on talk shows—that's the point. They are opinion shows. The best examples are *The O'Reilly Factor* and *Hannity and Colmes*. The news shows are about the news, and opinion plays no role. Of course, there are occasions on all networks when opinion does slip into the presentation of the news, but the viewers are smart and can discriminate between fact and opinion. And the viewers are bright enough to decide for themselves where they stand on an issue.

I have lived in Washington, D.C., for more than twenty-five years. This place is all about politics. That's the business of Washington. Conservatives and liberals, Democrats and Republicans have fought each other for decades, but often they have been personal friends. They can stand on the Senate floor and give passionate oratory about the North American Free Trade Agreement and then go out and enjoy dinner with their opponents. George McGovern says Bob Dole is a good friend. Ted Kennedy and Orrin Hatch reportedly play tennis. That's the way it should be.

Over the last few years that I've been in television I've met some hard-core conservatives, some of whom have challenged me, assuming I was a stereotypical white-wine-and-Brie liberal.

I like to listen to some of them really step deep into it for their assumptions about me and my political ideas. I can see them thinking, *Hmmm, educated lawyer in her forties (late, late forties), all those years on CNN, criminal defense lawyer—her position on Clinton's impeachment must have been because she is a liberal Democrat.* (In fact, I thought the Starr investigation was constitutionally misguided! High crimes and misdemeanors relate to professional, not personal extramarital, conduct. I never said I was in favor of his personal conduct—I was not—but merely that it did not meet the constitutional standard for removal.)

I have never publicly defined myself as a liberal Democrat or conservative Republican, but of course others believe they know what I think about every issue. I have seen both sides and had fun debating both sides.

Pat Buchanan once told me that he nearly fell over when he was reading a book and discovered my background. He was stunned that my father, who I adored, was Joseph McCarthy's campaign manager in 1946. People in Washington often make wrongheaded assumptions about your background, your education, everything you believe in. The fact is that nearly everybody in Wisconsin knows about my family's background, but the Beltway is a long way from the Midwest.

It's the truth. Appleton, Wisconsin, is famous and infamous for several things, not just Willem Dafoe and me, and one of them is Joe McCarthy. He was born on a farm near Appleton in 1908, a few years before my father, who was also born near Appleton. Joe was the fifth of nine children, and his parents were devout Roman Catholics. My father was one of thirteen children and was also from a Catholic family.

In Appleton, both my father and Joe were lawyers. They became good friends. They played, had fun, and yes, they were known in those early days as pranksters. Joe was the best man at my parents' wedding. In 1940 Joe ran for circuit judge and won.

When he was a candidate for the Senate in 1946, my father managed his campaign.

People have asked me about Joe McCarthy, but I did not know him. Of course he was discussed often in my childhood, but he died in 1957, when I was three. I am not sure if my memory is playing tricks on me, but I think I do remember him in our house one time when I was a child. That's it, though.

I know the many stories my parents told me about McCarthy. Some of them were pretty funny, some of them sad, and some of them very disappointing, given that he was a public official. Folks in my hometown talked about how McCarthy, who my father once described as having read one book in his life, had really gone off the rails in Washington in the 1950s. All of a sudden here was a guy who had been used to shooting his mouth off, except now there was television! There are so many things McCarthy said that in any other time might have been dismissed or ignored. Today, he would be reduced to the chatter of talk shows. His views wouldn't change the direction of national policies. But the new medium of television was hungry, and McCarthy was all too willing to feed the beast. It was almost as if TV was looking for the bad politician, and they found one. McCarthy's statements resonated, and they had effect. That was the problem. McCarthy was not ignored. He did not *want* to be ignored. And in truth, alcohol did not help Joe McCarthy. Alcohol and television have never been a good mix.

In my house we talked politics all the time. We argued, debated, and fought over the dinner table so much, it was like sports. The topics didn't really matter. What counted was that we could argue, disagree passionately, and still love each immensely.

I remember in 1974 when President Nixon's former law part-ner and attorney general, John Mitchell, was convicted on charges of conspiracy, perjury, and obstruction of justice in the Watergate scandal. Mitchell served nineteen months in a minimum-security prison in Alabama before being released.

I argued with my father that Mitchell should have served time in a maximum-security prison, something commensurate with the criminal convictions against him, instead of a cushy minimum-security facility.

My father said I was wrong. Mitchell had been the U.S. attor-ney general; he would have been killed by the hard-core inmates in one of those prisons. What would be the point in endangering the man's life?

Oh, I was adamant in my viewpoint, and he was calm in his delivery of his. I argued, Hypocrisy and favoritism! An easy life for white-collar criminals! Special treatment! I was unwavering.

Years later, of course, after I became a lawyer and spent time visiting clients in real prison, I came to agree with my father. I changed my mind. Mitchell was not given a death sentence by the judge, and going to a hard-core prison would have been one. A former attorney general in a hard-core prison would have been murdered. My youthful idealism conflicted with the practical reality of the situation. (Aging can do wonders for one's good judgment.) But both my father and I respected our differences of opinion. Frankly, he probably just thought I was a dumb kid, but he granted me the right to have my view.

My father taught us that even if you disagreed with some-one—even if you felt he was making a mistake—that didn't mean you should question that person's integrity or the fact he believed in what he was saying, even if it was wrong.

I recently reread Barry Goldwater's 1979 book, *With No Apologies*. Goldwater writes:

> Joe McCarthy was unquestionably the most controversial man I ever served with in the Senate. The anti-anti-Communists were outraged at his claims that some of the principals in the Truman and Roosevelt administrations actively served the communist causes.
>
> McCarthy was supported by a strong, nationwide constituency, which included among others, Joseph P. Kennedy, the father of John, Bob, and Edward. A variety of respected, credible federal employees disturbed by security risks in the national government provided McCarthy with a steady stream of inside information.
>
> The liberals mounted a skillfully orchestrated campaign of criticism against Joe McCarthy. Under the pressure of criticism, he reacted angrily. It is probably true that McCarthy drank too much, overstated his case, and refused to compromise, but he wasn't alone in his beliefs.

That's for sure. Now, I do believe that McCarthy was wrong. He hurt a great many people, and I'm not excusing that. But whatever you say about McCarthy, he was not alone in his beliefs. History is conveniently rewritten by some, and today you would think everyone was anti-McCarthy at the time! (It's kind of like the French—to listen to them discuss World War II you'd have thought every French person over the age of fifty was part of the Resistance!)

When I reflect on this difficult period of history, I also remember how adamant my father was about the business of mistakes—recognizing when you've made one, and learning from it. For him, it was not the end of the world to make a mistake. It happened to everyone. You just needed to fix the damage (and really fix it), whatever it was.

My father taught me a lot. One time when I was sixteen years old, after returning home and parking my father's car, I walked into the house and had some silly argument with my mother. I was probably having one of those I'm-mad-at-the-world teenage tantrums. My mother, choosing a really bad moment, asked me to get in her car, which was in the driveway, and go to the store to get milk or something.

I didn't want to. I had something better to do, like call my friend Amy Wallace and plan revenge on the nuns in our school. Anyway, I argued, yelled, and then stomped out of the house to go to the store.

Well, my mother's car was parked in our driveway. My father's car was in the street where I had parked it, behind my mother's car.

I got into the car, slammed the door, muttered, put the key in the ignition, threw the car into reverse, and roared out of the driveway.

Crash! I plowed my mother's car directly into my father's. Needless to say, the fenders of both my mother's and father's cars were significantly reorganized. We are talking very twisted metal here.

Slowly I walked back into the house. My father was on the

phone and hadn't heard the crash, and he waved at me to wait a minute till he hung up. I stood there in the den for what seemed three years. Then he hung up.

"What is it, baby?" (I was the youngest of three and always his baby.)

"Uh, I had a little accident."

"Hmmm. Which car?" he said.

"Um . . . kind of both of them."

We walked outside. My father and I stood there looking at the wreckage. He had his arm on my shoulder.

"Well," he said slowly, "it is sort of good this happened."

I thought, *What, is he crazy?* Both cars were wrecked and looked horrible!

He turned to me and continued: "You just got your license a month ago and you lost your temper. That could have been a child you hit, and it was just a car. Cars can be fixed. That's why we have insurance. Children can't be fixed. I know there will be times again in your life when you lose your temper, but you will never forget the sound of that crash, and because of that sound, you will never again lose your temper and then get behind the wheel of a car."

He was right. I'll never forget that sound. And I have gotten angry, but never behind the wheel. He taught me a huge lesson that day—and it wasn't a bad way to raise a kid.

Since September 11 we have seen a time of great patriotism in this country, which surely is a very good thing, and long overdue. I am making some assumptions about all of us as Americans, but here goes: We all support President Bush in the war on terror; we all pretty much think Saddam Hussein is a terrible guy who has been a brutal dictator to his people; and we all want to find Osama bin Laden and . . . well, I'll leave what we want to do to him to the imagination.

But there are legitimate disagreements about how to win the war on terror. Some reasonable people are concerned that we are paying too high a price, that we are giving up some of the precious liberties we have enjoyed since this nation was founded in exchange for investigating terrorists who live in our own land. We are facing some serious compromises.

Senate Democratic leader Tom Daschle was one of those who, in his role as leader of the opposition party, questioned the wisdom of some of President Bush's approaches to the war on terror and the success of the president's tactics. In November 2002 he had this to say: "We haven't found bin Laden. We haven't made any real progress in many of the other areas involving the key elements of al-Qaeda. They continue to be as great a threat today as they were a year and a half ago. So by what measure can we say this has been successful so far?"

He appeared on *On the Record* to reiterate his view: "I don't think anybody has a right to say we're winning the war on terrorism until we see more results."

Now, I don't care whether you agree or disagree with Tom Daschle—that's not the point. But in the first instance, all Daschle did was simply pose questions, propose a different view. Oh, sure, there was more than a touch of politics, but it was still an important question.

Boom! Mark Foley, a Republican congressman from Florida,

sent out a press release saying, "It appears his patriotism has gone away with his party's majority." Rush Limbaugh, on his radio program, began referring to Daschle as "Hanoi Tom." And letters soon began flooding Daschle's office addressed to "Tom 'Osama' Daschle." This was way over the edge—somewhat fueled by the fury that TV created.

The fact is, our leaders, whether they be Democrats or Republicans, have a duty to question the president, whether he be a Republican or a Democrat, without being called traitors!

I also have a right to disagree with Daschle, and here is where I do: Daschle was wrong to say, as he did on my show, that nobody has a right to claim victory in the war on terror. Says who? You may not agree, and you may have facts that point to the contrary, but of course you can say there is victory in the war on terrorism. The president or any other government official has a right to say we're winning the war on terror. For political reasons they had better be right or else they'll get pummeled in the next election. Since when do we tell each other what we can and cannot say? We are not talking the classic "fire in a crowded theater" standard here. These are opinions. We have a right to disagree, and Daschle shouldn't complain that the president doesn't have a right to say just about anything he wants to say. This is what I was referring to earlier when I sang the praises of our open society.

The whole tone of these silly exchanges is a perfect example of the kind of thing that cheapens all of us. I don't think Americans can afford right now to attack other Americans for questioning or probing public policy. The stakes are just too high.

I'd like to finish with a brief discussion again about my father, the guy who taught me about right and wrong, and about justice; who taught me to debate but not hate; who showed me how to accept mistakes and strive to become better; and who made me want to be a lawyer because he loved the law so much.

My father procrastinated. He was a procrastinator. I don't think he ever signed my report card on time. The nuns used to get surly at me when my report card was always—and I mean *always*—late getting back, but it was because of my father's procrastination. That's just the way he was. The nuns blamed me, but my father had his own clock.

Filing his state tax returns was no different from signing my report card. He was always late. But he always paid his state taxes, and he always paid the interest and late penalties that he owed— and there were plenty. You know how interest and penalties can pile up on money owed the state!

In 1983 my father was convicted of three misdemeanors (not felonies) for failing to pay his state income taxes on time. At the time he told me this had been his practice since 1939. My father argued to the state: "For many years I've been filing my state income taxes late, and because I am a state employee, you have all my withholding." He also pointed out that the state had his pension from many years of state service. He added that because he always paid the fines and penalties, the taxpayers of the state of Wisconsin, who paid his salary as a judge, had not lost a dime. Unfortunately, while it was indeed true that the state was not out any money from my father, the law did have a deadline for filing the returns even if money was not owed and penalties were paid. His late filing was a problem because he was a judge.

After a long fight, the Wisconsin State Supreme Court, as part of its role of exercising supervision over judges, gave him a two-year suspension from the bench for his late filing. That action in 1986 effectively removed him permanently from the bench, because within that two-year period he reached the state mandatory retirement age of seventy.

Now here is the problem as I saw it. My father made a mistake (or you could say he made the same mistake several times). Yes, of course he should have filed on time. The point is, he did something wrong and he was willing to pay the price, which he thought was paying fines, penalties, and interest. For years, nobody told him he couldn't do that. Nor did the state ever tell anybody else who habitually paid his taxes late that this was suddenly a terrible offense against the state. File late, pay the penalty—that was it.

By charging my father with these three misdemeanors for filing late, the state was arguing in effect that my father intended to defraud. They were arguing that he was a thief. It was difficult for me to understand, because how can you be a thief if you are paying the taxes plus fines and interest, a provision that Wisconsin allows as part of its state laws? It seemed like a stupid law. Who was hurt?

The misdemeanors broke my heart. My father decided to fight both the misdemeanors and the collateral civil proceeding.

But you know how slow courts can be. My father died in September 1989. Our hearing before the Wisconsin Supreme Court on the collateral civil matter was scheduled for January 1990.

Some people said I should just forget the whole thing. It was not a huge deal—the problems stemmed from three misdemeanors (which of course are minor offenses), and it did not involve much money. It would cost me more in airfares and expenses to go to Madison to argue the case before the Wisconsin Supreme Court than the case was worth to my father's estate. And, of course, my father was dead.

But I couldn't let it go, because I believed the state was wrong. My father had made a mistake, and he had paid the penalty. For the government to essentially call him a thief even after he was dead was just wrong. It just did not sit with me.

I'll never forget the day in January when I appeared before the Wisconsin Supreme Court. It was during a blizzard, the snow so deep and the wind blowing so hard that I didn't even know if I could make it into the building. I had never seen such snow— even the flight into Wisconsin the day before had seemed life-threatening. But I was determined to do this.

I must have looked a wreck when I finally walked into the Wisconsin Supreme Court. (Actually, a newspaper account from the time described my appearance as "the hair that denied knowing of combs." Even then!)

I stood up before the court on the little box they keep handy for short lawyers.

"My father was not a thief" was my first sentence. The justices of the supreme court seemed shocked. Those are not the usual introductory words to an argument. Usually you simply say "May it please the court" and then politely proceed.

Yes, I went on, my father had failed to pay his state income taxes on time; that was true. But he always paid them and the interest and penalties. And he had been suspended from the bench for two years for his late filing. To my mind, the state was going too far in saying he intended to defeat the income tax system. All of this I said without breaking eye contact with them.

One of the justices quickly interrupted me and said, "We aren't calling him a thief." But I didn't see it that way.

"If you rule against him, against the estate, you are," I said.

Associate Justice Shirley Abrahamson quoted the precedent of a 1947 case where a lawyer hadn't paid his taxes, ever. But she missed the point. My father had paid his taxes—just late.

I argued that the 1947 clause was not a precedent and didn't apply because my father had paid his taxes.

And on it went.

Four months later, in April 1990, the Wisconsin Supreme Court ruled in my father's favor. We had won. They did not reverse the misdemeanors, but on the civil matter they ruled that he had not intended to defraud the state's taxpayers.

There had been lots of talk when my father faced these misdemeanors. Many people liked my father, so they were upset about what they thought was an unnecessary use of state resources to go after him. Some people even had a theory about why my father had been prosecuted, since he was rumored to have been the only state taxpayer ever prosecuted for paying taxes late in Wisconsin. The state attorney general at the time was the great-grandnephew of former United States senator Robert La Follette Jr., the man who Joe McCarthy had defeated in the 1946 Senate primary, the campaign that had been run by my father. They called my father's tax problems "La Follette's revenge."

You know what? I never thought about it. I don't care and I never did. It doesn't matter. I can only hope that a personal disagreement over politics didn't lead to such a dreadful result. This is what I mean when I say disagreement about issues or tactics should never, ever turn personal.

I can only hope that the prosecution of my father was not done for political reasons. And yes, I have no doubt about it—he should have paid his state taxes on time.

Fairness and good judgment—not perfect judgment—is all my parents ever demanded of me, and that is all that I have demanded of others. That means my friends, my colleagues, my family, and my employers. Everyone.

P.S.: I do know my father would have been very proud of me for standing up for what I believe. He also—for me, and not for him—would have loved that I won.

5

THE SUPREME COURT
AND CAMERAS
IN THE COURTROOM

There should be a litmus test for Supreme Court and federal court judges, and that test should be their opinion about allowing public access to court proceedings. Let cameras inside the courthouse, or at least allow an audio feed to radio. What are they hiding?

SOME PEOPLE GET REALLY MAD ABOUT TAXES or traffic or food additives. I understand. But there is nothing that gets my blood boiling more than the fact that there is a group of people in this country whose decisions affect our lives and who get to do their work in secret. They determine outcomes for the most important issues of the day, from abortion to gun control. They even determined critical issues during the 2000 presidential election that ultimately affected who occupied the Oval Office. And yet they are allowed to operate away from the scrutiny of the American people. We can read their decision but the process is not completely open.

I am talking about the Supreme Court and the federal courts. I've always thought that folks who worry themselves about the Trilateral Commission and the question of who killed Kennedy should turn their attention to the Supreme Court instead. You want secrecy, cloak-and-dagger stuff, mystery, intrigue, shadowy figures accountable to no one? Forget Robert Ludlum. Try the Supreme Court. The highest court in the land is determined to keep the American people who pay their salaries from watching them do their jobs. To me, that's dangerous in today's world.

This Supreme Court is a particularly activist one. They're busy sticking their noses into every part of your life, make no mistake. For the first time since the New Deal in the 1930s, this Court has curtailed what Congress assumed to be its authority over interstate commerce. The Court ruled, for instance, that neither a federal gun control law nor the Violence Against Women Act had enough connection to interstate commerce to come under congressional jurisdiction.

This kind of stuff is a big deal. Telling an elected Congress to get out of the way ("overriding Congress," in more polite language) and telling elected state legislatures what they can and cannot do (as the *New York Times* put it, "insisting on having the last word") puts this Court squarely in your living room.

But even though the Court is in your living room—and your bedroom and workplace, for that matter—the justices don't want you in their office. They ban cameras from the courtroom, and they even ban audio! In other words, unless you want to travel to Washington, D.C.—and have the money to do so—there is no way for you to hear or know what is going on inside the Supreme Court. That is just wrong.

Nobody else in government gets to act this way. Even Pentagon officials have to give briefings to Congress. The entire legislative branch doesn't act like that. If you wish, you can watch Congress in session, debating issues, on C-Span. The president of the United States routinely gives televised press conferences and answers questions. He may not love it—who would?—but he does it because he knows it's part of the deal, part of the business of living in this American democracy. Why do federal judges get to hide from the American people? What's up with that? Who made them kings?

Now, you have to understand that the entire matter of cameras in the courtroom is a settled issue in all but a few states. And in virtually all states that allow cameras, it is a matter of discretion for judges on a case-by-case basis.

Let me give you a little not-too-boring history. Back in the 1930s the biggest trial of the day, the O.J. trial of its time, was the trial of Bruno Hauptmann for the kidnapping and murder of Charles Lindbergh's infant son. To look back at it now, it seems like something out of a bad black and white movie: huge bulky cameras, flashbulbs popping. The coverage was so sensational, disruptive, and over the top that the American Bar Association recommended in 1937 that photography be banned from courts.

Congress then enacted a rule banning photography or broadcasting in all federal criminal cases. (That law, called Rule 53, is still on the books.) Most states followed along. Until 1962 only two states, Texas and Colorado, allowed cameras.

In a 1965 case called *Estes v. Texas,* the Supreme Court overturned a criminal conviction, ruling that the cameras were too disruptive. Four of the five justices found that televising trials was inherently unconstitutional and a violation of due process.

Now skip to 1981. A different group of justices is sitting on the Court. In *Chandler v. Florida* they upheld a burglary conviction despite the fact that part of the trial was televised over the defendant's objections. The Court said it was not overturning *Estes* but rereading it in a narrower sense. The Court didn't blatantly endorse televising trials, but many states interpreted it that way.

Inconsistent? Well, maybe, but also with a nod to common sense. Important was the change in television and broadcasting technology. You didn't have big, noisy cameras anymore. There could be video and audio feeds in a courtroom and nobody in the court might even notice them. News organizations agreed to pool footage. In other words, you don't have to have more than a single camera or radio feed in a courtroom. Technology makes the whole business unobtrusive. The Court was right in recognizing this.

So far, so good. But as more states allowed cameras, the federal judiciary remained adamantly opposed to them. In 1996, testifying before a Senate subcommittee, Justice David Souter said, "The day you see cameras roll into our courtroom it's going to roll over my dead body." Justice Anthony Kennedy has said, "We are not part of a national entertainment network."

Now, come on. The dry, legalistic proceedings of the Supreme Court will, I promise, hardly be entertaining. And the justices know this. They know there are no theatrics involved at this level—you are not going to get crying witnesses and criminal outbursts in these courts. Robert Downey won't be appearing in the U.S. Supreme Court no matter how many drugs he takes, and Winona Ryder can clear out Wal-Mart if she wants to, but she is not headed for a date with Justice Scalia. There are no celebrities involved here.

So let's try to address the justices' concerns. What are they afraid of? Even if one were to imagine that cameras intimidate witnesses or scare jurors, there are no witnesses in the Supreme Court and no jurors. So scrap the silly excuses.

If the Supreme Court is worried about the security of the justices, don't put the cameras on the justices. Just show the lawyers. Show the arguments and open up the whole process. It is absurd to think that the justices fear the lawyers will grandstand, and here is why. In the United States Supreme Court a lawyer gets from fifteen to thirty minutes to make a presentation. What lawyer would possibly waste valuable time grandstanding? Believe me—and I know this is hard to do, since most people hate lawyers and refuse to believe anything they say, but trust me on this one—no lawyer is so stupid as to waste time grandstanding in the Supreme Court.

Did you also know that lawyers can't move while in the Supreme Court? They are ordered to stand at a lectern and make their presentation, and then they are told to sit down. A light on the lectern comes on to say that time is up, and you had better sit down.

I am even willing to compromise if those justices are still too nervous to show their faces. How about a live radio feed?

I believe the mystery that shrouds the Supreme Court and its decision making has really hurt us as a country, and I'll tell you why. Maybe the best example of the reach of their decisions and how divisive they can be is the 1973 *Roe v. Wade* abortion decision. That decision legalized abortion up until twenty-six weeks of pregnancy, and it was a decision that affected generations. But it did more than that; it created a politically explosive issue that today continues to haunt American politics. Men and women all over this country are elected to office or defeated based on their views about a woman's right to choose abortion.

Millions of dollars are spent by groups who want to protect legalized abortion, and millions are spent by groups who want to outlaw it. Radical antiabortionists have bombed abortion clinics, and some deranged people have shot and killed doctors who perform abortions.

Now, I am not saying that cameras in the Supreme Court would have eliminated controversy around abortion. I am not that naive. But I think it would have been good for everyone to see and hear exactly what the Court went through in coming to its conclusions. People would have been able to listen and think as they heard the judges struggle with the issue. Would it have changed minds? Maybe not. But perhaps we wouldn't have had doctors who perform abortions being gunned down or photos of fetuses paraded in protest marches. And maybe the pro-choice side would have been more understanding, at least, of those who oppose abortion. In other words, maybe we could have had more dialogue and less violence. I am not talking about televising their actual deliberations—just the lawyers' arguments and justices' questions.

Why should the American people not have been allowed to hear that argument live? Maybe, had we been able to see and hear exactly how the justices came to their decision, we would all be just a little less divided. Maybe the decision would have made more sense to the public.

The fact is that the Supreme Court justices do act like nine kings. They are appointed for life, so they fear no one. While they may be well intentioned, they've forgotten that they work for us and not the other way around. I am not in favor of doing anything that would diminish the importance of their job, but I *am* in favor of making the Court more accessible to the people. We own it. It is that simple. It should not be a cloistered branch of the government.

When Justices Kennedy and Souter make the kinds of state-ment cited here, they give the go-ahead to other federal judges to maintain secrecy in their own courts. It gives them permission, and it sets the example. The federal judges don't want to let the people see what goes on inside their courtrooms. The judges argue that it would create issues of decorum, result in unfair pro-ceedings, invite lawyer grandstanding, or intimidate witnesses and jurors.

"We're not in the entertainment business," parrots Chief Judge Edward Becker of the U.S. Court of Appeals in Philadelphia, as reported in the *San Francisco Chronicle.* "We have a solemn duty to ensure the fairness of every trial." So is he saying all state courts with cameras are a sham? Let's face it: Trials happen because peo-ple are mad at each other, or have committed crimes, or have been hurt in some way. Because they involve matters of crime or disputes between parties, trials are never pretty. But somehow state court judges are able to control the proceedings in thousands of courts all over America. Local television stations show trials all the time.

There is no evidence that televising court proceedings com-promises justice in any way. Indeed, the evidence points to the contrary. The convincing example is Court TV. That channel has televised more than a thousand state trials since 1991. Not one verdict has been reversed in the appellate courts due to cameras in the courtroom.

The bottom line is that many judges talk about the U.S. Con-stitution being a "living document" and reflecting the times. Shouldn't the court be a "living institution" and reflect the times? Cameras in Congress did not destroy democracy. They simply allowed the kindergarten teacher in Chicago to see where her tax dollars were going.

In a democracy, that should not be so scary an idea.

As of this writing, Senator Charles Grassley (R–Iowa) has introduced a bill that would give federal judges discretion to permit camera coverage. The Sunshine in the Courtroom Act passed the Senate Judiciary Committee on November 29, 2001.

6

HOW I BECAME THE POSTER GIRL FOR PLASTIC SURGERY

How you look is your business and nobody else's. Your looks and your life are not a democracy—not everybody gets a vote. Make your appearance and your choices a totalitarian regime—you are the boss.

LET ME TRY NOT TO PUT TOO fine a point on it: I have worked hard in my life. I worked hard in college and law school, got several degrees, worked at practicing law, worked at building a successful law firm. Then I started a second career as a television news analyst, and I worked hard at that too. I've worked hard at my marriage and have done everything in my power to be a good daughter and sister, the whole thing, okay? People thought I was pretty smart—or at least educated.

Then one day I had plastic surgery, and I became a bimbo to some.

When I went into television I tried to bring the same values and principles with me that I had lived by in my law career: the same attention to detail, passion for winning, desire for success, and commitment to fairness. This fair-and-balanced business is not just a slogan to me—I take it seriously.

Things were going pretty well. Then I decided to leave CNN and join the Fox network. So for the first time in maybe twenty years I had a month off from work. A month where I could sit around sporting my favorite look, which is a bathrobe with a down vest over it because I am too lazy to turn up the heat and too impatient to wait for the house to get warm. I could do absolutely nothing for the first time since high school if I wanted to. I had a whole month where I didn't have to get dressed up, act like a grown-up, and try to sound smart. This was my dream! I could be a bum! Frankly, it was the first time when the burden of responsibility seemed to be magically lifted from me and I could be whimsical—I could stay up till all hours watching movies and reading books. I did not have to worry about clients going to prison for life, or reporting the facts correctly on television, or getting the story first.

Now, you must understand what happened during that month, how a strange and very unusual silence descended upon the house. The cell phone stopped ringing at all hours. (One reason, of course, is that CNN pulled the plug on my company phone.) My pager didn't go off very often, and even the Black-berry took a snooze. As for me, I was happy! Totally content. Not dissatisfied with anything and certainly not worried about my career on television, because a wonderful new job was waiting for me just four weeks away.

Immediately after it was clear I would be leaving CNN, they pulled me from the air, because they didn't want my face on TV anymore and they wanted to thwart the momentum that Fox had built up. The first Sunday after CNN benched me I was reading the *New York Times* in my bathrobe and drinking coffee with my husband. That morning I'd caught a glimpse of myself in the bath-room mirror. *Hey, what happened to that sixteen-year-old?* I still felt like a sixteen-year-old in spirit—I like to have fun—but somehow I did not look sixteen years old. I took a closer look and discovered bags under my eyes. *Huh? Me, bags? Must be a mistake.* I took a closer look. Sure enough, there it was: the ordinary wear and tear that comes with age.

Hmmm, how about getting rid of those bags under my eyes? It was, I must emphasize, a whim.

I brought the subject up with John.

"Should I get rid of these bags under my eyes?"

"What bags?" (Right answer!)

"These."

"Honey, you are beautiful to me. Anything you want to do is fine," he said. (Again, right answer. He was two for two.)

"But what do you think?"

"Whatever you want." (Now I was a bit annoyed, as I wanted some advice.)

"I'm serious—what do you think?"

"Ask your sister." (A dodge, I think, but a safe response nonetheless.)

Through my sister, who is a doctor, I found a plastic surgeon in Washington. The doctor said that he had planned to be overseas that week doing charity work, but because of the terrorist attacks of September 11 his trip had been canceled. So in no time at all—two days—I was in his examination room. He explained to me during the exam that I actually didn't have bags under my eyes, although that was the way it appeared to me. What I had, he told me, came with age. I think the word he used was *trough,* which made me think of cows munching away on a Wisconsin farm. He recommended doing a very limited procedure—an eye tuck and the fixing of the troughs—and warned me that when it was all over, I might not notice that much had been done, though I could always have more done later. It would be an outpatient procedure, and there would be a bit of swelling for three weeks. Basically, no big deal. He said he could do it the day after next.

I did a quick mental calculation. I was due on the air at Fox in three weeks and three days. *This will work,* I thought. It'd be an outpatient procedure, so the swelling couldn't be that bad. (In my lexicon, the word *outpatient* translates to "no big deal and you live.") Plus, my mother was 100 percent Irish, and I too have the luck of the Irish. If everyone else was swollen for three weeks after this type of surgery, I would be swollen for fourteen days or less.

Most people seek second opinions before having surgery, but I did not. I have the luxury of my sister's judgment, and I was in a hurry. While I did not seek a second opinion about the actual surgery, there was one thing the doctor said to me that caused me to think twice. So on this one point I sought several opinions from my most trusted sources.

As I left his office, the doctor told me that I could not eat or drink the morning of the procedure. I said, as an afterthought, "What about coffee?" I figured no one would be so sadistic as to deny me coffee. He said, "No coffee either." I said okay but was scandalized. It also made me have second thoughts about this very respected and skilled doctor. I immediately called my sister.

"He said I can't have coffee."

"Of course you can't have coffee. This is surgery."

Suddenly I began to wonder about my sister. *What's her problem?* Yes, I am younger, and I accept the fact that she is the boss. But was this some residual power dynamic that had survived from our childhood? This was truly sadistic! What's the big idea about a little coffee? And since at least 1970 I have started every day with coffee. I was not about to break a good record now.

I needed to get a third opinion on the coffee issue. I called a surgeon friend and asked her.

"No, you can't have coffee. It is surgery."

For the first time, I thought, *What have I gotten myself into? Maybe this is a big deal.*

The day of the surgery I bounced into the doctor's office as if I were having my teeth cleaned. They said I'd need a ride home, so John waited . . . and waited . . . and waited.

A few hours later, out I came from surgery and recovery. I remember nothing. I was drugged and dazed. John took me home, but I recall very little about the ride. The next day, yes, I looked like a domestic violence victim, but I had no pain. A few days later I got on a plane to go to Florida. Why shouldn't I travel if I wanted to? It was my time off. The airline folks looked at me funny, so I explained, "I just had plastic surgery." I did not want anyone to think John had beaten me.

My debut on Fox was scheduled for February 4. Well, the weeks went by. Each morning I awoke, looked in the mirror, and asked myself, *When is this swelling going down? I have a drop-dead day, a national TV launch date. Where is my Irish luck?* I'd wake up, look in the mirror, and realize I still looked like the Pillsbury doughboy.

The day between the meeting with the surgeon in his office and the actual plastic surgery, I mentioned to Fox chairman Roger Ailes that I was having the surgery. For everybody who would later say that Roger Ailes had pressured me or wanted me more "glamorous," here's the truth: Roger told me there would be swelling! Roger is a TV guy who has been dealing with talent for years. He knew a lot more about plastic surgery than I did. And of course I didn't listen, since I had no idea what swelling really was. He said he just wanted to warn me. He had hired me based on my record and how I looked at the time that he offered me my own show, and he was neither expecting nor desiring anything else. I promised him I'd be ready for the launch of the show, that the surgery wouldn't interfere. I was determined to keep my word. (And, of course, I did.)

I had one major flaw in my thinking as I calculated the three weeks of anticipated swelling. I never thought about—and this is really stupid for someone who has been in television for almost ten years—the fact that I needed to shoot promos before the launch of the show. You can't sneak a show onto TV—you have to promote it big time. Obviously, we'd have to shoot promos before the February 4 launch date. Hence I would have to be ready for prime time, at the latest, two weeks after my surgery. It was then that I realized I'd really stepped into it this time. I had not and did not intend to hide my plastic surgery. After all, the whole point of doing it was to look different. But I also didn't want to start my new job at Fox looking like the folks at CNN had beaten me up before they let me go.

Well. The last week in January, I headed to New York to do some promotional television spots for the new show.

"I'm still a little swollen," I warned Roger on the phone.

In New York, at the Fox building, I walked into Roger's office. Roger is very direct. He took one look at me and said, "Do you want to delay the show? If you want, I'll delay the launch."

Okay, so I looked pretty bad. You can't keep ice cubes in your pocket all the time. Now I really was looking at myself in the mirror every hour, hoping that the swelling had miraculously gone down. But each time I looked, I seemed more swollen. My mother's Irish luck was letting me down.

"No," I said. "I'll look a little funny for a while, but the viewers can get beyond it. I promised I was showing up for work, and here I am." After all, I was about to launch a show based on issues and debate, using all my years of legal expertise and training, right? So what if I was a little puffy? I was hired to do a news talk show, not a beauty tips show.

And so that's how my big "going public" with the plastic surgery happened. I asked the advice of a few friends and colleagues, including my coauthor on this book, who at the time was covering the war in Afghanistan. "So I think I'm going to have to go public and talk about the plastic surgery," I said.

"Oh, Greta, just shut up about it," Elaine rasped over the satellite phone from Kabul. "Don't say anything. Nobody will notice or care." *She must be right,* I figured. *Why would anyone have any interest in what I might do to my face?* (Remember that Elaine was in a war zone, where a little puffiness under the eyes was, shall we say, the least of her worries.)

Well, the day after my first promo aired, using what is called a "video grab" (a still photo that is taken from a live television picture), the *New York Daily News* bannered my new mug across the top of its front page under the headline "Foxy Babe." I confess, I thought it was pretty funny. I was sort of amused at how I'd gotten myself into this mess. I guess idle time can produce curious results.

The headlines were followed by cartoons. My favorite was the

CBS eye logo all dressed up and some remark about me starting a trend. It made fun, but it was funny and got a laugh out of me. I had done something on a whim, and suddenly I had become the poster child for plastic surgery.

The media avalanche had begun. Two weeks later I was on the cover of *People* magazine. So much for those journalistic instincts from my colleagues in the business.

Everybody had an opinion.

"Fox hired a tomboy and they got a babe. It's all everybody was talking about," Michele Greppi, national editor of *Electronic Media,* told *People.*

Some people insisted I had had more than my eyes done.

"Nobody looks so different from eyelid surgery alone," declared Dr. Pamela Lipkin, a New York City plastic surgeon. (My thought: No, Dr. Lipkin, most people don't go on television or allow their swollen faces to appear on the cover of one of the country's most popular magazines within three weeks of plastic surgery.)

This stunning development in the history of the Western world also provided a wonderful opportunity for everyone to weigh in on how I'd looked *before* the surgery.

"I thought she looked like a senior version of Kiefer Sutherland," Cindy Adams wrote in a column completely devoted to my face. "Understand, we are not talking Jennifer Lopez here. She's not fall down, drop dead, fabulous, sexy, to die. Not like Britney Spears has to worry. But she looks nice. I mean, the better to interrupt everybody."

Or how's this from Robin Gerber in *USA Today,* in a piece

headlined "Why Turn Brilliant Lawyer into Barbie with Brains?": "Van Susteren had been physically transformed to approximate the idealized woman that Fox viewers expect. She looked anything but courageous. Van Susteren is a reminder of the minimization of American women by American culture."

The entire world seemed to have something to say. There were even stories in the British press! The London *Independent* ran an article under the headline "And Finally . . . the True Cost of Being a News Babe."

A Nexis search shows that between February 2002 and February 2003, there were 193 references in the media around the world concerning my eye surgery.

And then there were the viewers! You have to remember that the Fox audience didn't know me at all. Most of them do not, and did not, watch CNN. When the show debuted, all the Fox viewers really knew was that I was some lawyer from "liberal" CNN. If they knew anything else, it was probably some misperception that I thought O.J. Simpson was a great guy and was innocent of murder. So I think it's fair to say that many of them weren't exactly enthusiastic about me in the beginning. Nonetheless, the Fox viewers were fantastic about the surgery. They judged me, all right, but they were ready to judge me based on what I said and how I presented myself.

The fact is that I did not set out to make a big stand on cosmetic surgery. I wasn't taking an official position on behalf of American women one way or the other. I never intended to speak out in favor of or against plastic surgery, and I wasn't looking to become an authority on notions of beauty in America.

While some have called me "brave" and "courageous" for being up-front about it, having plastic surgery is a far cry from either of those things. Frankly, I think Katie Couric is brave and courageous for taking on the topic of colon cancer. I have never met her, but I admire her because her goal was to save lives, and I believe she has. I just stumbled onto the plastic surgery scene, and I certainly didn't do it to make it easier for others. If it did, and if others feel better about themselves after they've done it, then sure, I'm pleased. But, in all candor, that was an accident.

I had eye surgery because I wanted to. Nobody told me to. I didn't think I was ugly, and I certainly wasn't insecure about the way I looked. I did it because I felt it would help me look better, and I wanted to look better *for me*.

If someone had told me to do it—my husband, Fox, or any-body else—I would have taken one look in the mirror and told them to go jump in the lake. I am stubborn that way. I really don't like being told what to do. I make my own decisions on just about everything, from my political views to my physical appearance.

A few people said some really outrageous things to me about my surgery. One reporter for a major media outlet asked if I thought the surgery would affect my credibility. Huh? Because I was candid and didn't hide it, I now have a credibility issue? Does that mean if I lied and hid it, I would have more credibility? What a riot! It's pretty weird to be second-guessed by the news media because you *didn't* lie about something. Anyway, I politely answered—since it's never smart to pick a fight with the media—that the plastic surgeon had merely fixed my eyes, not removed brain matter or deleted my education or my news experience.

Of course, it was also amusing to me that the media were so

interested in my plastic surgery. While I won't name names, I certainly was not the first by any stretch of the imagination. No one told me it was supposed to be a big secret. I somehow did not equate plastic surgery with bank robbery and thus a need to keep it quiet.

Another New York magazine editor commented that she thought I had "sold out the sisterhood," as if cosmetic surgery somehow made me not a feminist or a supporter of women's rights. That is simply ridiculous. The women's movement is supposed to be about choice and freedom, the right to make your own decisions. I certainly wouldn't tell someone to have cosmetic work, and I would have been horrified if anyone had told me to. Though sometimes I think my unkempt hair distinguished me more to viewers than anything else, I have made my own choices about my appearance, and anybody who thinks otherwise has obviously never listened to me for five minutes.

Several months after the surgery I happened to be in a green room (the waiting area at TV stations where guests congregate and drink coffee before they go on the air) with Patricia Ireland, who was then president of the National Organization for Women. A lot of reporters had called NOW for comment right after the surgery, but they always declined to say anything. I wondered about that, because I suspected there were some angry feminists ready to pounce on me. "So, Patricia," I asked her, "how come you and NOW gave me a pass on the eye surgery?"

I loved her answer. "Well, Greta, you had a track record."

I did have a track record, in the courtroom, in the classroom, and on television. And that is how anybody, male or female, should be judged: by what you do, how you live, who you are. It is that simple. Appearances are important, but nothing is a substitute for doing your homework, getting an education, working hard. That is true even in television: Viewers are not stupid and they recognize credibility when they see it (even with bags under your eyes!).

7

NO PATIENCE WITH
POOR EDUCATION AND
NO TOLERANCE FOR
ZERO TOLERANCE

School should be a positive, life-defining experience. Education inspires, challenges, even provokes students. It encourages them to question. But our educational system needs to get back to the basics. Kids need to learn math, reading, history, and geography before they consider studying origami.

ANYBODY WHO KNOWS ME KNOWS THAT I AM a bit strict about grammar and about the basics of education. Some say the fact that I am in total agreement with Lynne Cheney on these matters makes me a conservative.

Since when did being passionate about reading and writing define one's political bent one way or the other?

The vice president's wife has been a guest on my show several times, and we have found ourselves in major agreement about the need for education reform. Mrs. Cheney, of course, is not just the vice president's wife. She is an expert in education and holds a Ph.D. in British literature from my very own alma mater, the University of Wisconsin.

During a speech not long ago to a group of government officials, Mrs. Cheney put it this way: Too many educators believe rote memorization of dates and facts is bad for students. Without a framework of basics, she said, many students have little or no grasp of history, geography, and the humanities.

I could not agree more. A recent national study found that 57 percent of high school seniors were unable to identify "important people, places, documents and ideas in American history." Only

20 percent could recognize passages from the Gettysburg Address, and many thought Ulysses Grant was a general in the American Revolution.

That is outrageous, but it is the kind of thing I hear from high school teachers all the time. Some tell me that many students think Europe is a country and that few kids can do math without a calculator.

That kind of ignorance will not make America strong and competitive in the world. In some areas of education we are actually being surpassed by other countries. Progressive educators' idea to add more "user-friendly" courses was aimed at getting students more involved and also making subjects more relevant. But some high schools actually offer electives such as Health-Enhancing Physical Activities, a course designed to teach kids that exercise is healthy (what a revelation). And a school in Connecticut offers an elective called Changing Person (that is really what it is called—I don't even know what that means), which they say is a course about "personal awareness" and "total wellness." I still don't get it. I do get that it does little to provide a fifteen-year-old with a good education.

To be fair, we are doing better in this century. First of all, let's give ourselves credit where credit is due. Our schools are better than they've ever been. In 1900, according to census data, only 11 percent of kids fourteen to seventeen were in school, but by the end of the millennium, the statistic had mushroomed to 93 percent. And 83 percent of the adult population were high school graduates. But we can do better still. I say forget the self-esteem classes taught in California. You want to feel good about yourself? You'll have plenty of self-esteem when you can read and write and master an English vocabulary that puts you at the top of your class.

We need to encourage teacher certification programs to make sure our teachers are the best. I want to put my support behind people like Amy Jensen and Linda Rodrigo, two teachers in Lancaster, California, who proudly earned their profession's highest standard: certification by the National Board for Professional Teaching Standards. The two were the third and fourth instructors in the Antelope Valley to achieve that distinction following a yearlong application process.

"It is a rigorous process," said Jensen, who teaches second grade, speaking to the *Los Angeles Daily News*. "It took hundreds of hours. . . . It was a sacrifice to do."

"It's my proudest professional accomplishment," said Rodrigo, who teaches first grade.

And you know what? The state of California will reward them with a one-time cash award of $10,000 each and then $5,000 annually for four years. But I'm willing to bet it wasn't the money that made them want to be the best teachers they could. Certification isn't an easy process. Instructors must submit two videos of themselves teaching in their classrooms. Then they analyze the literacy skills and growth of two students over the course of a year. They submit lesson plans and take essay tests. Certification has been achieved by about twenty-four thousand teachers nationwide, including about two thousand in California.

Now imagine if that was your teacher when you were a kid. Imagine knowing that your teacher was writing his own essays to become better at his job. Wouldn't that kind of diligence make you want to be a better student too?

ZERO TOLERANCE . . . NOT

We all know the times have changed since the good old days, whenever *they* were. Nowadays kids have access to guns. They can trade in drugs whose names we can't even pronounce. They sport a familiarity with profanity and sex that we didn't. The games weren't as rough, and they weren't played for keeps.

And, of course, there were no incidents such as Columbine. There just didn't seem to be the fury that could turn a kid murderous, the kind of rage that could make two middle-class kids want to blow up a school.

Growing up in the '60s in Appleton may sound pretty tame by today's standards, but you'd be surprised at the mischief we got into. We had our bullies and our misfits, and there was a lot of acting out. There were threats, fights, and risks taken that no sane adult would want a child to take. But we survived, as much for our failures as for our successes! Kids need to be able to make mistakes, pay the penalty, and move on. In New Jersey recently, fifty kids got suspensions for parroting curses and threats, the kind of things they heard their parents say at home. And these weren't hulking teenagers—these were kids between five and eight years old. Those little kindergarten "thugs" now have police files on them!

Here's another story: Recently, an outraged teacher urged police to charge two ten-year-old boys for their prank of putting soapy water in his drink. Sure, these kids had to be disciplined, but they were charged with a felony that carried a maximum sentence of twenty years. These are ten-year-olds!

Who is being protected here? Zero tolerance began as a congressional response to students with guns, but gun cases are the smallest category of discipline cases now in schools.

Zero tolerance has been expanded to mandatory expulsion for threats of violence, disobedience, defiance of authority, profanity, disruptive behavior, and possession of drugs or alcohol. That can cover a lot of misbehavior! Threats are a big part of zero tolerance, and of course threats can be broadly defined. In some schools the list of banned "weapons" includes manicure kits.

Zero tolerance is a one-size-fits-all policy that doesn't take into account the kid or the nature of the offense. Kids know that one size doesn't fit all, and they know that different offenses can't be met with the same punishment. A childlike threat or prank, however mean-spirited, just isn't the same as doing real harm to someone else, and it doesn't warrant the same punishment. It's unfair. What are we teaching our kids about fairness, justice, and understanding? What message are we sending?

The reaction to school violence has gone too far. We have to use common sense here. According to the U.S. Department of Education, 90 percent of school systems have zero-tolerance policies for violence or threats. Imagine the nine-year-old nerd in the back of the classroom getting suspended for threatening to shoot a wad of paper at you. Or another nine-year-old getting suspended for threatening to get back at him! Well, it's happening. Kids are being suspended and redefined as criminals. In the 1998–99 school year, over eighty-seven thousand kids were expelled from schools nationwide. That's over eighty-seven thousand kids we've now essentially pushed out of the system, eighty-seven thousand young people we've put at risk. Twenty-six states require alternative schools for suspended or expelled students, but there is little information about the quality of alternative schools. Some may be great, but are they all?

There is something else. According to a U.S. Department of Education report, it is minority kids who are most often suspended or expelled. Zero tolerance doesn't weed out the middle-class misfit with a rage to blow up his classmates, and it can't safeguard us against future Columbines. What it does too often is stigmatize the minority kid. Once a suspension is on the record, it's in the police computers. If an inner-city kid is suspended and then hanging out on the street with his pals, it's a good bet he'll get stopped, checked, and then hauled in. He's already marked.

Who suffers when the school community becomes a virtual police state? We all do. The biggest casualty will be education itself. Say goodbye to excellence. Zero tolerance, by definition, is not a preventative; it's a reactive measure. Zero tolerance does not ensure education or guidance. It does not support better teachers or foster opportunity for kids to build relationships with positive role models. It does nothing to assist kids in dealing with unsupervised free time. At the end of the day, it encourages kids who misbehave to get a whole lot worse, to have more opportunity to hang out with other "bad" kids, and to model their behaviors in increasingly antisocial ways.

Zero tolerance tells kids, "Do as I say, not as I do." But everyone knows kids watch what we do more than what we say—they model themselves after us. Kids will, in essence, do as zero tolerance does and become better bullies. They will learn that justice is meted out by force. They will learn to avoid authority. They will not struggle to form their own values. They won't learn how liberty comes in the asking of questions, and they won't strive to be entrusted with that liberty.

Bottom line: Teachers and schools need to use good common sense—not overreact and not underreact.

A FINAL WORD ON A GREAT TEACHER

How do you make a good teacher? He has to be well paid, of course, but also supported by the system.

Let me tell you another story. This time it's about Miss Duprez, the teacher who ran my study hall. Miss Duprez had enough dignity not to endure any of my juvenile insolence. She was tough on me, and she got me to shut up when I laughed inappropriately. That woke me up. I admired her.

The following year she offered to let me "skip" study hall. She gave me an opportunity to show that I was trustworthy—an opportunity to trust myself.

As Miss Duprez and hundreds of other good teachers have demonstrated, moments of insight and illumination—those light-bulb moments—don't happen by rote and can't be prescribed. A good teacher has to be patient, creative, and flexible, able to spot the moment when an individual student is open to learning something new. The teacher has to keep experimenting with information, bringing what's current and relevant in kids' lives into the classroom. And a good teacher has to be willing to give kids the opportunity and gift of responsibility.

Education reform won't happen by trying to restructure

school bureaucracies and by getting tough on students. It will happen through teachers' and parents' fierce advocacy of better education. School administrators and parents have to give teachers support, government has to give them the resources, and all of us have to care.

8

HOT COFFEE, PERSONAL RESPONSIBILITY, AND GOLD CHAINS

The Twisted World of Lawyers and Torts

Tort reform . . . isn't. When companies or people make mistakes and hurt people, they have a responsibility to fix the hurt. Not to buy a new yacht for the injured party, but to fix the injury they caused. So for quicker and cheaper resolution of civil cases, reform the "hourly-rate" lawyers and watch how quickly the parties settle.

WHAT'S A TORT?

A VERY INTELLIGENT NONLAWYER friend of mine recently said, "Greta, I gotta be honest. I'm not even sure I know what a tort is, but I'm gonna assume it's not Viennese pastry." Thank God I have nonlawyer friends.

Let me immediately give you an example of a tort and then an example of tort reform.

Linda McDougal, forty-six, was diagnosed with an aggressive form of breast cancer in May 2002. Her doctors recommended a radical treatment, a double mastectomy. The St. Paul, Minnesota, woman decided to go ahead with the surgery. Why wouldn't she? She wanted to live, and the double mastectomy was a way to treat this cancer.

Two days after she had the surgery in June, McDougal's doctor walked into her hospital room. "She had bad news," McDougal told CBS News. "She didn't know how to tell us other than to tell us, and immediately I thought I was dying. And then she told me I didn't have cancer."

United Hospital's laboratory had mixed up McDougal's biopsy results with another woman's. The pathologist who made the mistake is still employed. Frankly, unless he or she is likely to make that mistake again, that person should probably remain employed. The question as to continued employment is whether steps have been taken to make sure it will never happen again.

"I am maimed for the rest of my life," said McDougal, adding that she has had several infections and must still undergo several reconstructive surgeries.

That is a tort: a negligent act that was committed against Linda McDougal. Sometimes these acts are negligent and sometimes they are intentional. In the case of Linda McDougal, as tragic as it is, it appears to have been negligent. No one deliberately wanted to hurt her, but she still deserves to be compensated.

Earlier this year, President Bush borrowed an idea from a 1975 California law and proposed a $250,000 liability limit for pain and suffering damages in tort cases. (Don't ask how he came up with that figure; he has never explained the formula for it. In fact, it is completely arbitrary.) No matter what happened to you, no matter who was responsible, no matter what the evidence that a company or individual knew beforehand that you might be hurt, $250,000 is the limit for pain and suffering that the wrongdoer must pay to compensate you.

Before I get further into this, a couple of definitions. When you are hurt and win a case against the person or organization responsible for your injury, you can be awarded two types of damages: punitive and compensatory. Compensatory damages are intended to make you whole, and punitive damages are intended to punish the wrongdoer when the conduct is deliberate.

Here's an example: If you were made a quadriplegic as a result of someone else's negligence, you would get an amount of money as compensatory damages for your medical bills, your lost wages, for the loss of the quality of your life, and the pain and suffering. Certainly there is greater pain and suffering with full-body paralysis that will never correct itself than from, say, a broken arm that will heal with no permanent damage. But under the proposed tort reform, the most you could get for the pain and suffering is $250,000 regardless of the injury.

That is tort reform: establishing a blanket cap of $250,000 for pain and suffering.

Linda McDougal's breasts were removed by an act of medical malpractice. Under President Bush's plan, a jury could not award her more than $250,000 for pain and suffering. After legal fees, what is McDougal left with for the loss of two breasts?

Does that seem fair to you? It might be—but why is Congress deciding this? Should it not be the people in the community, the jury? It does not seem fair to me that Congress determines how much this woman is hurt—they have never met her!

Torts are civil wrongs recognized by law as grounds for a lawsuit. These wrongs have caused injury or harm to some individual, and constitute the basis for a claim by the injured party. Now, we all know how litigious our country has become, and how a lot of so-called injured people will claim whiplash if they think they can get away with it. And that's where tort reform comes in—it's a way to put a ceiling on litigation run amuck. That sounds reasonable, doesn't it? Not! You'd be surprised what a stir tort reform has caused.

They used to say the way to really ruin a dinner party was to talk religion or politics. Oh, for the good old days! If you want to experience a radioactive conversation and start the dinnerware flying, bring up tort reform. For real entertainment, try to make sure there are some lawyers in the room, and at least one or two people who have been in car accidents.

You can hear the screeching from one side of the room: "Frivolous lawsuits, clogging up the judicial system!" "Those damn lawyers, fleecing everybody!"

And from the other side of the room comes: "Oh, sure, let the corporations off the hook!" "Big business owns Washington."

No one feels ambivalent.

Frankly, I don't feel ambivalent either.

But before I jump into this shooting match, let's look more closely at what torts are and what they are not—and why any of this matters to you.

Torts, for starters, is not a branch of the law that was created to decide who is bad and who is good. No one goes to jail in a tort case. From *Black's Law Dictionary*:

> Tort: (from Lat. *torquere*, to twist, *tortus*, twisted, wrested aside). A legal wrong committed upon the person or property independent of contract. It may be either (1) a direct invasion of some legal right of the individual; (2) the infraction of some public duty by which special damage accrues to the individual; (3) the violation of some private obligation by which like damage accrues to the individual.

Torts is an opportunity in the law for responsibility to be decided and assigned. It is not an us-against-them topic. In theory, it is an area of the law where we can resolve differences, compensate for our mistakes, and be compensated—much like a confessional allows for cleansing of personal error.

The whole issue is whether we should allow Congress to put a ceiling on what your injuries are worth. Should we tie judges' and jurors' hands in deciding what the appropriate damages are in a civil case?

PERSONAL RESPONSIBILITY

Let's say I back into your car in a supermarket parking lot. I was distracted, thinking about something else—it doesn't matter, because I know I hit your car. But I don't drive away. I try to find you and give you my name and number so I can fix it—make you whole.

It is called personal responsibility. Do I wish I had not hit your car? Of course! I feel awful. I feel stupid and incompetent as well, and my day is pretty much ruined. But do I really want to be a jerk and run and hide? No. Does it mean I am a terrible driver and nobody should ever get in a car with me? No. It simply means that on one occasion, for whatever reason, I made a mistake. I want to get past this and do the right thing. Let me compensate you in full.

But only for what's appropriate. Only for your fender, pal. You can't say that your 1720 Stradivarius violin was smashed or that the lens of your Hasselblad camera got cracked unless you can prove it was really there and damaged as a direct result of the accident.

And don't claim weeks later that Granny was asleep in the backseat and is now in a wheelchair. Your fender and your lights—whatever your actual damages were—are all I am going to pay for.

As a right-thinking person, I assume that corporations and their executives feel the same. If the company hurts people—accidentally, of course—I assume the executives want to make those people whole. Why would a company and its executives want to hurt and run?

It's hard for me to believe—and I don't—that people at Ford said, "Hey, isn't it great that we know there's a defective transmission in our cars that throws the car into reverse . . . but let's not tell people." The fact is, we may never determine how much they knew about the car's poor design. But what I do know is that it took an award of $4 million in punitive damages for the company to redesign the transmission. Also, did Ford honchos sleep well in the 1970s when they knew the Pinto would burst into flames if it was hit? I don't know, but it took a $125 million punitive-damage verdict to get the car's fuel tank redesigned.

We've recently been hearing about the lawsuits against fast-food chains for causing obesity. Yes, you're right to scratch your head in utter perplexity, because most adults know that a regimen of cheeseburgers, chocolate shakes, and fries is neither healthy nor slimming. But think a minute—what about the obese child who goes to a fast-food restaurant on the way home from school every day? What about the vending machines inside schools that only offer junk food? Where are the parents? I get indignant over parents who wallow in ignorance and do terrible damage to their kids by not teaching and encouraging them to eat a reasonable and healthy diet.

However, I also think responsibility is *shared* by fast-food restaurants that deliberately market to kids and lure them to their outlets as often as possible with all kinds of ploys: toy giveaways, playgrounds out in front, cartoonish mascots, and other gimmicks. They must share in the responsibility because kids are vulnerable, and the law protects children from the greed and stupidity of adults.

In some instances the responsibility for damages is shared by both the person who gets hurt and the person who does the hurting. The best example of this is when a speeding car runs a red light and plows into a car driven by someone who is not wearing a seat belt. Both have some responsibility. The first driver should not have been speeding and should have stopped at the red light, and the second driver should have been wearing his seat belt to minimize the harm done to him in an accident. States have two potential ways to address this, and in my opinion, one is fair and the other is not. Some states permit shared responsibility, which is called comparative negligence. Comparative negligence allows for everyone involved to share in the responsibility when appropriate—that seems fair. I think it would be fair to reform all state laws to conform with this idea.

Other states have a different type of statute, known as contributory negligence, which I believe is not fair. In such a state, if you are 1 percent responsible and the person who hit you is 99 percent responsible, you can't recover anything for your loss. In the example above, if it is determined that the driver not wearing a seat belt was contributorily negligent, he will recover nothing in a contributory-negligence state but has the opportunity for some recovery in a comparative-negligence state. In a comparative-negligence state, for instance, if it was determined that not wearing a seat belt was 20 percent of the problem, the damages would be reduced by 20 percent. Hence both drivers share the responsibility. That seems fair, doesn't it? Good reform would permit fair sharing of responsibility in those states that do not currently do so.

Okay, I know that was a bit painful and might seem overly legalistic, but it gets me back to the theme that runs through this whole book and my whole life: fairness. I look for it everywhere. And to me, personal responsibility is a big deal when it comes to fairness. Personal responsibility is a very popular theme in our country now, and that's good. Except that those who support so-called tort reform seem to think there are exceptions when it comes to making up the damage after you have done something, accidentally or intentionally. They think there should be an arbitrary ceiling on damages, all agreed upon beforehand. Here's a recent example from North Carolina that will explain what I'm talking about.

Last January there was a plane crash that killed twenty-one people in Charlotte. The plane's pitch control elevator was malfunctioning on eight flights before the fatal crash, but the maintenance people somehow didn't fix it. So it crashed the ninth time. I think that caused the accident, yet the NTSB has not released a final report. Under President Bush's plan, each family would receive a maximum of $250,000 for pain and suffering. I think it's awfully difficult to simply hand over a $250,000 check to each of the families of the twenty-one dead people and expect them to go away.

A cap on damages is way too simple, and not fair. Damages should be appropriate to the harm done. One price doesn't fit all.

Plus, if it turns out that the company was more than just negligent—then the issue of punitive damages should be considered. The company will need to be "punished" so that it "learns" not to do that again.

HOT COFFEE

The classic case for those calling for tort reform concerns McDonald's coffee. This case got a huge amount of media attention, but most of it was of the slap-and-run variety. "Millions of Dollars Go to Dummy Who Didn't Realize Coffee Was Hot" was the implied headline in most of the coverage of the lawsuit. The McDonald's case became—and still is—the poster child for runaway verdicts. That's understandable if all you know is that McDonald's got sued for serving hot coffee and some woman got a million-dollar verdict. Of course that seems ridiculous! Shouldn't she have known that coffee is hot?

But I wonder if any of you ever heard all the facts or what happened in the end. No one is in favor of frivolous lawsuits or outlandish results; however, it is important to understand some points that were not reported in stories about the case. The reason this matters is that the strongest voices in favor of tort reform always turn to the McDonald's hot-coffee case as an example of a jury verdict run wild. And that is simply not true. If we allow tort reform—I actually call it "tort deform"—to proceed, we will lose the ability as citizens to recover damages from big corporations who manufacture faulty products (and sometimes know it) and thus endanger lives, or against doctors and hospitals who make mistakes that they simply should not have made. In other words, don't forget Linda McDougal. Here is a summary of what really happened in the McDonald's case, courtesy of the American Trial Lawyers Association and reproduced in the Lectric Law Library, an online legal service:

Stella Liebeck of Albuquerque, New Mexico, was in the passenger seat of her grandson's car when she was severely burned by McDonald's coffee in February 1992. Liebeck, seventy-nine at the time, ordered coffee that was served in a Styrofoam cup at the drive-through window of a local McDonald's.

After receiving the order, the grandson pulled his car forward and stopped momentarily so that Liebeck could add cream and sugar to her coffee. (Critics, who have pounced on this case, often charge that Liebeck was driving the car or that the vehicle was in motion when she spilled the coffee; she denied it.) Liebeck placed the cup between her knees and attempted to remove the plastic lid from the cup. As she removed the lid, the entire contents of the cup spilled into her lap.

The sweatpants Liebeck was wearing absorbed the coffee and held it next to her skin, which made the resulting burn more severe. A vascular surgeon determined that Liebeck suffered full-thickness burns (third-degree burns) over 6 percent of her body, including her inner thighs, perineum, buttocks, and genital and groin areas. She was hospitalized for eight days, during which time she underwent skin grafting. Liebeck, who also underwent debridement treatments (removal of dead or contaminated tissue), sought to settle her claim for $20,000, but McDonald's refused. Her original claim is key—why didn't McDonald's simply pay her medical bills? Given all the time she spent in the hospital and the gripping pain from burns, she was gracious in not asking to be compensated for her pain and suffering.

Since McDonald's would not settle, she sued.

During discovery, the portion of the pretrial where the defendant must turn over many of its internal memos, McDonald's produced documents showing more than seven hundred claims by people burned by its coffee between 1982 and 1992. Some claims involved third-degree burns substantially similar to Liebeck's. The documents proved that McDonald's had extensive prior knowledge about the hazard that its coffee presented to its customers.

McDonald's also said during discovery that, based on a consultant's advice, it deliberately held its coffee at between 180 and 190 degrees Fahrenheit, for at this temperature the coffee maintained optimal taste for the longest possible time. The consultant admitted that he had not evaluated the safety ramifications of doing this. Other establishments, such as Denny's or Burger King, sell coffee at substantially lower temperatures, and coffee you serve at home is normally 135 to 140 degrees. Further, McDonald's quality assurance manager testified that the company made sure that coffee was held in the pot at 185 degrees, plus or minus 5 degrees. He also testified that he was aware that a burn hazard exists with any food substance served at 140 degrees or above, and that McDonald's coffee, at the temperature at which it was poured into Styrofoam cups, was not fit for consumption because it would burn the mouth and throat. The quality assurance manager admitted that burns would occur but testified that McDonald's had no intention of reducing the holding temperature of its coffee.

The plaintiff's expert, a scholar in thermodynamics, testified that liquids at 180 degrees will cause a full-thickness burn to human skin in two to seven seconds. Other testimony showed that as the temperature decreases toward 155 degrees, the extent of the burn decreases exponentially. Thus, if Liebeck's spill had involved coffee at 155 degrees, she most likely would have avoided a serious burn.

McDonald's testified that customers buy coffee on their way to work or home, intending to consume it there. However, the company's own research showed that customers intend to consume the coffee immediately while driving. It's far-fetched to think that coffee obtained in a take-out restaurant would not be consumed in a car.

McDonald's also argued that consumers know coffee is hot and that they want it that way. The company admitted its customers were unaware that they could suffer third-degree burns from the coffee and that a statement on the side of the cup was not a "warning" but a "reminder," since the location of the writing meant that it would not be sufficiently visible to serve as an adequate warning of the hazard.

The jury awarded Liebeck $200,000 in compensatory damages. This amount was reduced to $160,000 because the jury found Liebeck 20 percent at fault in the spill. She had to share some of the responsibility. The jury also awarded Liebeck $2.7 million in punitive damages, which equals about two days of McDonald's coffee sales.

Interestingly, postverdict investigation found that the temperature of coffee at the local Albuquerque McDonald's had dropped to 158 degrees Fahrenheit. Hmmm. Could this mean that

McDonald's lowered the temperature of its coffee after the verdict? I think so.

The trial court subsequently reduced the punitive award to $480,000—or three times compensatory damages—even though the judge called McDonald's conduct reckless, callous, and willful. However, no one will ever know the final ending to this case because the parties eventually entered into a secret settlement that has never been revealed to the public, despite the fact that this case was litigated in public and subject to extensive media reporting.

Here's why the McDonald's hot-coffee case is so important: Everybody supporting tort reform uses it as a blatant example of an excessive jury verdict. In fact, it is a perfect example of just the opposite. First, the woman did not get millions. She got $160,000 in compensatory damages and an unknown amount in punitive damages, but I'll bet it was way less than $480,000. (And $160,000 was a lot more than the $20,000 in medical expenses she initially asked for. By refusing to be decent and pay her hospital bills, McDonald's ended up paying for pain and suffering, loss of wages, and legal fees.) Yes, this is a substantial amount of money, but it is not millions, and there is no way it is the runaway verdict most people think it was.

Besides, every judge in this country has the power and the authority to reduce verdicts. A judge, presumably educated and experienced, sits there in a checks-and-balances capacity. If the jury is out of its collective mind, the judge can and should reduce the amount of the verdict. In this case, the judge did reduce the verdict. But that judicial reduction was not sexy news, so it did not get the attention the alleged millions did. So—you never heard this.

Of course, I don't think executives sat around the boardroom thinking, *How can we burn little old ladies?* But they took a business risk, weighing injury claims versus the profitability of keeping coffee longer. Now that their coffee had badly—and unnecessarily—burned Stella Liebeck, they had to take responsibility and make her whole. It cannot be ignored that with seven hundred prior claims, McDonald's sure knew there was a problem.

It was established that McDonald's knew the coffee was dangerously hot but kept it at that temperature in order to stretch the time they could keep it. By holding the coffee longer, extending the time it could be served, they saved money by not having to use additional coffee. In other words, they did it out of greed, knowing that someone might be hurt but apparently making the business judgment that it would be financially more advantageous to pay off claims from injuries.

At this point I would have thought McDonald's would have said, "Okay, we screwed up. We'll pay." But no! They resisted compensating this woman! And they knew that her burns were significant. When she got out of the hospital, she simply wanted her medical bills paid. She didn't even ask for compensation for pain and suffering—and she did have plenty of both.

Here's my guess about what happened. First, for business reasons, McDonald's wanted to maintain the practice of keeping coffee very hot. Second, the lawyers are paid by the hour and have an incentive to generate endless litigation. And third, the insurance company likes to make money and not pay it out. So they said "No deal" to a settlement.

What makes me angry about all this—and what should make you angry too—is that corporations are using the phony issue of tort reform as a shield to avoid responsibility. If a hospital laboratory makes a mistake so grievous that a healthy woman's breasts are removed, it should pay. By refusing to do the right and honorable thing, the corporations or hospitals or insurance companies have ended up costing themselves more in the courts, and then they cry "Foul!" at jury verdicts. Wrong. They can't have it both ways.

THE BAD GUYS . . . AND THERE ARE REAL BAD GUYS

I think there are five main culprits in the tort game: the insurance industry, what I call the "hourly-rate lawyers" who work for the corporations or insurance companies, the plaintiffs' lawyers, the judges, and the media. No one gets off the hook with me— except the people who serve on juries. And the funny thing about this? Tort reform is meant to "correct" the juries, and they are the only ones who are doing their job! That's pretty stupid.

Here's what happens behind the scenes when you get hurt. The corporations involved immediately notify their insurance carriers. The insurance carriers contract with outside lawyers who get paid by the hour. This is a red flag signaling that protracted litigation could be on the way, because if the case is quickly resolved, the lawyer and the law firm make very little money. The whole business of an hourly rate is a disincentive to handle the case quickly, since the lawyer gets paid regardless of success, and thus there is a huge incentive to stack up hours, whether he wins or loses. The longer the case drags on, the more the civil defense lawyer makes.

Worse, I doubt these hourly-raters even realize that they are doing it. They see themselves as being strong advocates for their clients, the insurance industry, but I think they never step back to look at what the cost is to the court system. And even more importantly, they fail to recognize that their greed hurts American citizens. Because if tort reform passes Congress, if the public falls for the idea that runaway verdicts are at fault, then you and I lose, not only as potential victims but also as jurors, because we will have lost the right to fairly compensate victims of negligence. I once had former House Speaker Newt Gingrich on my show, and he was talking about tort reform and how much it would help the system. During the break I said, "Newt, don't you realize the hourly-raters have a huge incentive to blow up a claim and make it a massive lawsuit? In many instances the hourly-raters have an enormous incentive to drag the litigation on rather than pay the full and fair compensation at the get-go. This creates havoc for the court system." He stopped, looked surprised and thoughtful, and responded he had never really looked at it that way. And I believed him.

Of course, when we went back on the air he stuck to his guns.

BUT WAIT! HOW ABOUT FRIVOLOUS LAWSUITS?

Now, I don't want to let anybody off the hook here, even with my bias favoring lawyers. This is not to say there are not ridiculous cases brought to court—there are! We have a lot of nutty people in this country who seem to find even nuttier lawyers to handle their cases. You hear so much about these, you would think there was an epidemic in our courthouses.

It's not true. You hear about the ridiculous cases only because sensationalism sells. How boring it would be to report that someone was truly hurt by a corporation and that the corporation resolved the matter quickly and in the most responsible fashion!

But the problem is that there is an incentive for those bad lawyers out there. To get cases, some of these guys will often make very unrealistic estimates to prospective clients as to what a case is likely to bring. For instance, assume you came to hire me to handle an injury case and I gave you my opinion that I thought I could recover $100,000 for your injury. When you interview other lawyers, you will find the next one saying, "She says she can get you a hundred thousand? Hah! Thats ridiculous. Your case is worth five million."

Which lawyer are you likely to hire? I know—the one who says he can get you all the money. So now what happens? Creating the most ridiculous expectations in order to secure the case fosters an environment of litigation, not one of resolving the case reasonably. You are not going to get that amount of money, but the lawyer will get your business.

Of course, ridiculous claims for money in the face of obvious negligence do create a problem for the most responsible companies and insurance defense lawyers. While I urge the hourly-raters to make sure their motives are pure, to settle the cases that should be settled and to do so quickly and not run up the legal bills, sometimes they have no choice but to defend a corporation that is getting blackmailed by a ridiculous claim. And if a plaintiff's lawyer has poisoned a victim's mind into thinking that a claim is worth millions, even a negligent corporation must fight the claim. It is about fairness and responsibility. Your lawyer is really unlikely to get you that absurd amount from the corporation or person who wronged you.

One of the problems of the media reporting only the sensational cases is that people get a very skewed idea of what reality is. Everyone thinks punitive damages are commonplace. They are not. Punitive damages are awarded only in the most outrageous cases and where companies knew or should have known that someone would get hurt. They are not awarded when a mistake has been made—that is where compensatory damages are awarded. Punitive damages are designed to punish the wrongdoer and not to compensate the person hurt.

Here is a fact: Major punitive damages are rare. A report by the Bureau of Justice Statistics and the National Center for State Courts that looked at 1996 state court data in the nation's seventy-four largest counties showed that punitive damages are awarded in only 3.3 percent of cases won by plaintiffs. The median amount of punitive damages was—are you ready?—less than $40,000. And juries are even skimpier than judges. Juries awarded a median of $27,000, while judges awarded $75,000. In other words, a jury of your peers is not going to be so willing to help you win the lottery.

People criticize plaintiffs' lawyers, calling them greedy. Yes, some are. Some are not. Some are simply trying to right wrongs. That is fair and right.

None of this is helped by the image of too many plaintiffs' lawyers. Let's face it—a lot of them look outright gaudy when they get out of their courtroom suits. You know what I'm talking about: There are way too many gold chains dripping from these guys' necks. I have read articles about one rich lawyer hitting golf balls into the ocean for his daily pleasure. There is a "million-dollar club" for those who have won verdicts in excess of $1 million. When they look and act that gauche, it's a real challenge to appreciate their craft or to understand their value to their suffering clients.

In truth, of course, it's the few rather than the many. The press (and I say this as one of them) seizes upon these flashy characters, making it seem like all plaintiffs' lawyers look like Mafia dons.

BUT WHAT SHOULD WE DO?

Reform the practice of paying hourly rates for lawyers in tort cases. This cannot be done by Congress but must be done by the corporations and the civil defense lawyers. Here is an idea: salaried lawyers for the defendants and defendant corporations instead of the unlimited hourly rates contracted out to private firms. This will diminish the incentive to litigate, litigate, and litigate. It will create an atmosphere of "Is this worth sitting down and resolving?" In the end, it will be cheaper for corporations and the insurance industry.

As for plaintiffs' lawyers' fees, I am a huge fan of the contingency fee. This means a lawyer takes a percentage of the reward at the end if and only there is a recovery. If there is no recovery, the lawyer gets nothing. This compensation plan gives lawyers an incentive to resolve quickly and smartly. How many plaintiffs' lawyers are going to get into protracted and dumb litigation when they know they stand a chance of making nothing at the end? Very few lawyers have the means to do that. They're making a living like everybody else, not playing the lottery. It puts the client and the lawyer into a partnership where both share the risk. In some instances the contingency fee can be as high as 40 percent—but in simple cases the client can and should negotiate that amount to something less. The fee should reflect the risk the lawyer takes and the estimated amount of work. Congress needs to get the message that what clients pay their lawyers is none of their business. A frequent topic of discussion is putting a statutory limit on the percentage of an award that can be earned by lawyers who represent victims. You can't in all fairness put fee limits on what victims can pay their lawyers and yet put no limit on what corporations pay their lawyers. Not only is it unfair to the lawyers, but the victims get hurt—it guarantees an uneven playing field, since the corporation will "overlawyer" the victim.

Make the judges work! There are remedies for wasteful litigation—judges can throw the frivolous cases out and even punish the lawyers who bring them. It's called Rule 11, and any judge has the right and the duty to throw out a frivolous lawsuit. Pressure them to have the courage to do it! They can also fine the attorneys for bringing a wasteful case to court in the first place. You slam a lawyer a few times with a financial punishment and the lawyer will change.

THE GOOD GUYS: THE JURY, WHICH MEANS YOU

In my view, everyone gets very poor marks here except the juries. And it is my absolute belief in the jury system—which means the citizens of our nation—that leads me to condemn tort reform.

Tort reform implies that you, the juror, are too stupid to properly assess who's at fault and how much damage was caused. The tort reformers believe that it's all too complicated for you to understand. Instead they think that Congress—which is thousands of miles away from the case and which has not heard one lick of evidence in the courtroom, seen the victims' injuries, read the corporate records, or heard the backgrounds of the parties—should get to arbitrarily decide on the limit for damages. That doesn't make sense. This is really no different from preferring the diagnosis of a doctor who has neither seen nor talked to the patient over one who has the patient in his or her examination room.

So what makes Congress so much better at diagnosing and understanding torts than the American people in the courtroom? Answer: money. Having Congress pass tort reform strips the American people of their jobs as jurors and satisfies the insurance industry's powerful lobby.

The jury—which has been so demonized by cynics in the media and by the insurance lobby—is made up of people like you. If you have ever served on a jury, you know that jurors try their best and make decisions based on what information is presented to them.

Bottom line? The problem is not the American people who get drafted to serve on juries. We are neither too stupid to understand a case nor likely to overcompensate a plaintiff with unreasonable damages. As citizens serving on a jury, we are doing our job and do not need to be "reformed" by the power of influential money. Let's keep lobbying money out of America's courtrooms. And speaking of lobbying, maybe we should take a look at who is pushing so hard for so-called tort reform.

9

FUN

Fun isn't a curse word. It's actually quite serious business, as it makes the hard times livable and the sad times bearable. Fun (appropriately, of course) should be part of a work environment too! Stuffed shirts and snobs who can't stop and laugh at themselves should be banished!

LET ME TALK TO YOU ABOUT A VERY serious topic. This is a weighty matter that I try to focus on as often as possible. It is an issue that I do my best to bring to every single one of my personal and professional endeavors.

I am talking about the grave topic of fun. Yes, fun, with a capital *F*. I can't tell you how often it strikes me that most people don't seem to be having any fun. They have forgotten how important it is. And they can get very mad at people who *are* having fun.

Now, before you say something like, "Oh, sure, *you're* on television making lots of money. Fun is easy for you," let me tell you that fun has nothing to do with money or success. Fun has to do with having the ability not to take yourself too seriously. Take your work seriously, take matters of health and family and national security seriously, but for God's sake don't take *everything* seriously.

Back when I was thinking about leaving CNN, I spent many difficult days trying to decide between an offer from Fox News and a new offer from CNN. I loved CNN, and I respected the men and women who actually put the shows on, but the atmosphere had become painful to me. When AOL decided to lay off people, they did so by calling in security guards. People were summoned into various offices, told they were being laid off, and advised to pack up their belongings by the end of the day, all under the eye of the guards. Can you imagine people who had devoted their lives to a company being treated that way? Every day I went into the CNN offices in Washington, D.C., to find more colleagues packing up. There were empty offices and sad faces everywhere. People who depended on their jobs for mortgages and health care coverage for their families found themselves out in the cold. It was horrible, and the atmosphere was constantly grim.

When I went to New York to talk to Fox executives, the atmosphere was completely different. People were laughing, making jokes. Secretaries smiled. The mailroom guys waved at me. They had cookies in the green room. (CNN in its budget cuts had even stopped serving snacks to guests.) Fox was a news operation, of course, but people were clearly having fun at work.

CNN finally presented me an offer that in dollar figures beat Fox's offer—by a lot. I told CNN, "Don't you get it? This is not about money. Don't you understand? I am not having fun here anymore. I can't stand what AOL is doing to CNN and its people, and I can't stand the atmosphere there. You are treating people like garbage. There is no fun at all. Are you going to change that?"

The CNN brass was incredulous. I don't think anybody had ever mentioned fun in a work environment in a contract negotiation. But to me, fun has got to be a part of work life. I know work is serious and every day isn't going to be a laugh riot, but it simply isn't healthy to be miserable every day of your working life, no matter what. Ask someone who has the most tedious, repetitious job in the world—somebody who works on a factory assembly line, for example—whether he likes his job. He may not like the actual work, but any longtime employee will tell you that what makes the job bearable is usually fun of some sort, especially with coworkers who are also having fun.

Someone asked me recently what I really consider fun. The answer may make you think I am even dopier than you thought before. It's not skiing or going to parties. It's not playing tennis or golf. I don't do any of those things. My idea of fun is . . . doing nothing (unplanned time).

Now, maybe you think when I was a kid I had other ideas. Nope. One of my oldest friends—we knew each other in kindergarten—is Amy Wallace, and we still talk all the time. You know what we did for fun as kids? We just talked and laughed—and always about stupid things, nothing of great consequence. More than forty years later, we still do the same: talk and laugh—and about stupid things. It is free and takes no planning. We just do it. It is doing nothing except enjoying good laughs and good company.

WE'RE IN TROUBLE NOW

Now let me give you an example of another kind of fun, and one where I got in some trouble with certain unfun Washington stuffed shirts as well as my viewers.

Every couple of months I get a really bright idea, one of those "Gee, this could be interesting and fun and it won't be a big deal" moments. (You remember, just like that quick, whimsical, low-profile plastic surgery decision a few chapters back.)

The genesis of this particular brainstorm was a plan for a quick trip to Los Angeles to tape *The Tonight Show* with Jay Leno. You might find this hard to believe, but I don't really like doing interviews, either TV or print. It feels weird to be the center of attention, and besides, I like asking the questions! I also wonder, why would anyone be interested in me? But everybody tells me it's good publicity for our show, so what the hell. I also don't like being away from home, so I try to cajole my husband, John, into going with me whenever I can. (Besides, John is the most fun person I know.)

My producer, Beth, knew I was going to LA, so she told me, "You gotta interview Ozzy Osbourne. At his house. We'll set it up. It'll be great."

Huh? All I knew about Ozzy Osbourne was . . . well, practically nothing. I have always considered myself cool—I did listen to Jefferson Airplane and wore bell-bottoms when it was right to do so in Appleton—but the truth is the years have piled up and I have neglected some of the necessary training for remaining cool, such as listening to music recorded after 1972. I'm not so cool anymore. Being cool takes some work and, well, somehow I forgot to work at it.

Beth, on the other hand, who lives in New York and knows everything you are supposed to know, did her best not to roll her eyes at my extreme unhipness. She informed me that *The Osbournes* was the hottest show on MTV. In fact, it was the hottest show ever on cable television, drawing in something like six mil-

lion viewers. The show was about his family. I got some tapes of
The Osbournes and went home.

Frankly, I thought Beth must have the facts wrong. How could
a show on cable draw six million viewers? How could a weekly
show have those numbers when it was only a reality show about
a family? I found out pretty fast that this was no ordinary family.
This was the Osbournes.

I did what Beth told me. (See, I can be obedient.) First I
watched the tape. I admit, it was not exactly normal TV. Ozzy
curses and is baffled by modern technology, such as the VCR.
Kelly, the daughter, has purple spiked hair and curses at her
mother. Mom Sharon gets mad at the neighbors and pitches a
baked ham over the fence. They are weird. But I'll tell you what
hit me most: The Osbournes seemed like a lot of fun, so I decided
to interview them.

Believe me, neither Ozzy nor his wife, Sharon, was what I
expected. So what did I expect? I don't even want to tell you. My
thought going into the interview was simply this: burned-out
rocker with wife. Period. That was what I was expecting and not
much more. Boy, was I wrong about this one.

Instead I fell in love with both of them. They were gracious
and funny and seemed completely unimpressed with all the fame
and truckloads of money coming their way. They were just about
to sign a deal for a rumored $20 million for their second season
on MTV. They were on the cover of *Rolling Stone, Entertainment
Weekly,* you name it.

"How long do you think you can keep this gig going?" I asked
Sharon.

"Hell, I don't know. But we're gonna milk it for all we can while we can!" she said. I loved that. She wasn't taking this fame and money stuff seriously.

Now, she and Ozzy take raising their children seriously. When Kelly got a small tattoo, Ozzy was upset; he doesn't think kids should get tattooed. "Did you do that to be different? You want to be different?" he asked her. "Everyone has a tattoo. Be different. Don't get a tattoo." Sharon was even more negative, but she also asked her daughter point-blank, "Did you do that because you were angry at something? Are you angry?"

But as for the rest of it? They were having a blast.

At one point, as we were setting up all the equipment for the interview, a studio light came crashing down. It landed right on a glass table, which broke with a heart-stopping sound. The deafening sound of the light pole going through the glass provoked dead silence among all of us in the room. We just stared. Had this really happened? Had a Fox News spotlight just impaled Ozzy and Sharon Osbourne's coffee table? Joel Kaufman, one of my colleagues, quickly said, "Uh, sorry. We can replace that!"

Without missing a beat, and with his deadpan straight-ahead stare, Ozzy said, "Well, you'd have to go back to the eighteenth century." Turns out we had broken a rare antique. Now, I can assure you that a lot of Hollywood people would have reached for their cell phone and hit the speed dial for their lawyer before a full minute had passed.

After the interview, and after having thoroughly enjoyed them, an idea hit me: How about taking the Osbournes to the White House correspondents' dinner, the most prestigious annual media party in Washington? I needed something to spice up the party. I thought they would be fun! Well, I was right about that.

There is a precedent for wild and unusual guests at the dinner, usually of the Hollywood celebrity variety. So why not bring the Osbournes? The dinner is always attended by the president of the United States. Maybe they'd even get to meet President Bush.

I and some folks from Fox worked on putting my table together. A few people turned us down, as Congress was on holiday that week. But by the night of the dinner my table was set, and it included Senator Jon Corzine from New Jersey and Senator Debbie Stabenow from Michigan.

Then I got a bit nervous that the senators would be stiffs and worried that they would be sitting with an unpredictable rock star, so I told them the Osbournes would be at the table. "Fine," they both said. "Sounds like it'll be fun!" added Senator Corzine. Now *there's* something rare in a politician! I immediately liked them both. I don't really care or know how they stand on issues. What I liked was their ability to be open to anything.

John, Mr. Fun himself, told me for days leading up to the event that his dream was to get on MTV and get bleeped. I ignored his juvenile comment, hoping that my fifty-five-year-old lawyer husband had higher aspirations in life. Every time he said it, I wondered, *What have I done?*

We were told an MTV crew would shoot everything except the actual dinner, as cameras were not allowed in. Afterward we would go to the Bloomberg party, the very chi-chi, hard-to-get-into soiree that follows the dinner and is held across the street at the Russian Federation, a beautiful old mansion.

The first hint of the night ahead of us came as the limo pulled up to the lobby of the Washington Hilton Towers. There were the four of us in Ozzy's limo (Ozzy, Sharon, John, and me), plus the MTV film crew. The car felt a bit like a tuna can, as there were more of us than there were seats. When the crowd saw the Osbournes, pandemonium broke out. The people went wild—fans, regular people, and more media than I have ever seen in Washington. It was a mob scene: flashbulbs popping, camera crews angling for position. "Ozzy, how do you like Washington?" "Ozzy, are you going to meet the president?" and even a few comments along the lines of "Hey, Greta, how you'd get the idea to bring Ozzy?" To say it was surreal understates how bizarre it was. I worried that the crowd in its efforts to see Ozzy would crush to death Federal Reserve Board chairman Alan Greenspan or one of the military generals standing in line to get into the affair.

Suddenly this idea seemed more bizarre than the one to have plastic surgery. Just exactly what had I been thinking? Was I nuts?

We finally made it up the escalator to the ballroom. Security was very tight, as it is any time the president is attending an event. I expected even tighter security than usual, since this was post–September 11. But we were whisked through metal detectors and seated inside the cavernous ballroom, some 2,700 seats at 260 beautifully set tables. What was unusual was that we were all alone—the only ones sitting in the ballroom.

The security people had brought us inside because Ozzy's presence was causing too much of a ruckus to control outside. Can you imagine? Six of us, sitting in our evening clothes in an empty ballroom?

WASHINGTON, D.C., LOOSENS UP

Staid old Washington went wild for the Osbournes. The *Washington Post* wrote, "In spite of itself, this segment of capital society went as crazy as the rest of the country." As soon as the ballroom opened, and throughout the dinner, our table was surrounded by fans wanting Ozzy's autograph. And when I say fans, I mean congressmen like Dennis Kucinich, White House staffers, and journalists. I have to say that I looked around at some of the other tables and they seemed a little, um, subdued. Our table . . . well, it was far from dull, to put it politely. Our table manners were severely handicapped by the fact that somehow we had twelve people eating at our table, though each table was set for only ten. To show what a good sport she is, in the face of "manners adversity" Senator Stabenow picked up the butter fork to eat with when she discovered she had no dinner fork. Someone who is not a good sport would have shown annoyance . . . but not the junior senator from Michigan.

I too was shorted in the silverware department and ended up using my butter knife to try to cut meat, since one of my dinner neighbors snatched my steak knife before I could act. Senator Corzine, a freshman senator and a former chairman of Goldman Sachs who spent millions to win election, laughed at the hullabaloo over a rock star and said, "Well, this gives me real perspective. Nobody cares about me!" Our table was laughing, sharing food. I finally said, "This doesn't feel like a political dinner. It feels like Thanksgiving at home!" The only thing missing was the debate over politics that always erupted at my family's dinner table. That was the fun and magic of the evening: a wild rock star, so incongruous in this setting, and a couple of politicians who were letting their hair down. Everyone forgot about politics and differences and just decided to laugh.

Then President Bush took the stage. Our mouths nearly fell open as he began his welcoming remarks.

"Washington power brokers, celebrities, Hollywood stars, Ozzy Osbourne . . ." The crowd laughed as he continued. "The thing about Ozzy is, he's made a lot of hit recordings: 'Party with the Animals,' 'Sabbath Bloody Sabbath,' 'Facing Hell,' 'Black Skies,' and 'Bloodbath in Paradise.' " The president paused for effect. "Ozzy, Mom loves your stuff."

With the reference to former First Lady Barbara Bush, a very familiar person to the audience, and the acknowledgment, Ozzy jumped on his chair and threw our president a kiss. *Uh-oh* . . . I froze, not knowing what was next. But Ozzy behaved himself and turned it into a great moment. People in the room—a room that included Washington big shots and journalists, Greenspan, Harrison Ford, Glenn Close, the ambassador from Afghanistan, and a healthy smattering of currency experts from the World Bank— began chanting, "Oz-*zy*, Oz-*zy*."

Ozzy is a phenomenon, as is the success of his show. But there were a good number of crinkled noses and appalled looks by some serious journalists at the dinner, who were shocked, shocked at the spectacle of it all. The *New York Times* called Ozzy the dinner's most "ridiculous" guest. (But the *Washington Post* called me "ingenious" for inviting him. Thank you!) An editor from *People* magazine said the whole thing was "undignified," and a few big-shot journalists who shall remain nameless thought Ozzy in the same room as the president was "tasteless."

Whoa! It was a p-a-r-t-y! We are not talking about bringing Ozzy Osbourne to the The Hague for the war crimes tribunal. We're talking about dinner.

WELL, THE VIEWERS WEIGHED IN ON MY NEW HIPNESS

To: ontherecord@foxnews.com
From: Rick in Kihei, Hawaii

Aloha, Greta. I always knew you were cool, but backstage at the presidential bash with the great Ozzy—wow. That was excellent. Truly hip. Rock on.

To: ontherecord@foxnews.com
From: Chuck in Elora, Tennessee

Greta—if someone had told me back when you were defending Clinton—I hated you then—that one day you would be my favorite pundit, I would have thought they were crazy. But Greta, you are now officially my favorite pundit. Why, you may ask? Because you invited the Ozz to dinner. I think that was the bravest thing anyone has ever done. I apologize for everything bad I ever said about you and now I will defend you every time people at work dog you out.

To: ontherecord@foxnews.com
From: Eric in Milford, Connecticut

Three cheers for Greta inviting Ozzy to the press correspondents' dinner. It was wonderful to see politicos act as fans.

But I have to be honest. Most of my viewers were really critical of my taking Ozzy to the dinner. I can't print the e-mails here because—let's just say they didn't use "family language." I got called some "serious" names. I think those attitudes are a shame, and I do think those people need to lighten up.

The bottom line was that it was a great night and a lot of fun for us, the Osbournes, and all those congressmen and reporters who came to get Ozzy's autograph. Life is short. Keep the important things in mind.

Just a few weeks later Sharon Osbourne was diagnosed with colon cancer and began a grueling six-month regimen of chemotherapy. When I found out about it, I was even happier that we had thrown caution to the wind that night and enjoyed ourselves.

But you know the real surprise? George W. Bush. He was a great sport. He had fun with Ozzy being there. He knew how to let his hair down. All those stuffy, dignified Washington journalists who were scandalized by Ozzy should take a hint from the president. Have some fun!

10

SPORTS, FAIRNESS, AND COMPETING FOR THE HIGHEST SCORE

Vince Lombardi was right: Winning is the only thing. But he forgot to add one caveat: It's everything only when you play fair and when the playing field itself is fair. Sports play imparts values to our kids; athletes are role models, and they need to remember that. Do the right thing and remember that kids are watching and maybe even imitating you.

THE FIRST PLACE WE LEARN TO PLAY fair and disagree without bloodshed is in sports. *On the Record* has aired a lot of sports-related shows. During my TV career I've done shows about football, about the responsibilities of players and owners, about baseball, and even about golf.

Boy oh boy, did I talk about golf and Tiger Woods one night (and I'll get to that later). But first . . .

Maybe some of you might think it's unusual that I'd love doing shows about sports. Is it because there is a perception that some women are disinterested in sports or aren't up to covering them on prime-time television? Well, let me tell you straight out—I love sports! And I *love* talking with people about them.

It's because I love competition.

Besides, things that happen in the world of sports do matter in our lives. Sports give people a reason to have a common goal—to win, of course, but also to be avid about fairness, excellence, and the pleasures that come from team support and community spirit.

It's an important part of human nature, and an important outlet for us all, male or female. Sports are not just for men!

I USED TO BE AN ATHLETE . . . KINDA

I like to think of myself as a great athlete. I was a star player in a tee ball league in Appleton, Wisconsin, in the 1960s. I had my dream position: pitcher. And let me tell you, I watched a lot of girls in the 1960s strike out as I racked up trophies for my star pitching!

Okay, okay, I know. Some of you familiar with tee ball realize that the ball sits on a chest-level tee and the little kids just swing madly at it. The pitcher doesn't actually throw the ball. So yes, it is true that the peak of my athletic career involved standing there on the pitching mound, doing nothing. All I needed to do was wait for the other kids, the ones with the bat, to wind up and strike out. (A little like hosting a television show with certain guests, when you come to think of it.) My team won many Appleton citywide championship trophies. Like all those record albums for which I've not had a turntable in twenty years, the trophies have moved with me from apartment to apartment to house to house for decades. I can't part with them. You just can't toss out trophies, can you? They sit in storage right next to the albums and my high school uniform.

I confess that memory has greatly enhanced my athletic prowess. The truth is, I have not played sports in ages. I still boast about my skiing, but I haven't gone down a slope in more than twenty-five years. I figure that the adage "Quit while you're ahead" works just fine. (Now, of course, if you hear me talk about skiing, you'd think I was heading to the Winter Olympics.)

Unfortunately, my body has not kept up with my embellished memory, but that's never stopped me from having great fantasies about my athletic talents. And that's what sports are about for most Americans. We're not playing sports as much as we're watching them and fantasizing about our youth and the athlete we should have been.

WHAT SPORTS DO FOR US

Sports ground you in your body (okay, even if it is just a *fantasy* of whacking it out of the park). They ground you in your home team, in your community. There's something vital about sharing in the excitement, the thrill, of a good fight with the people around you. Some might say that's just our baser impulses getting the better of us—but look again: What's a good lawyer, a good doctor, a good chess player, but someone who is drawn to a challenge and is hell-bent on winning?

Sports allow us to have our contests and conflict without real bloodshed. Conflict is a big part of being human, and I think there's a lot of necessary pleasure we get from outsmarting, outplaying, outpsyching our opponents. Just ask me about my Nielsen ratings, that great scorekeeper of American television. I love ratings—they're one way I measure how well I can best my competitors and whether the viewers are happy. So what about ratings and sports? My competing for viewers is no different than a NASCAR driver flooring it as he heads into the final curve. In broadcast, the final curve is sweeps. In cable, it is the monthly numbers. It is exhilarating to hear the crowd, and the ratings are television's crowd. They indicate that you have done your job well.

Contests come in many forms, not just on the field. Sports

provoke dialogue—a verbal contest—on many social issues. Fairness is always at the scrimmage line where sports are concerned. Should college sports money be divided equally between women's and men's sports? Are doctors more interested in getting an injured player back on the field than getting him proper medical care? Has the game itself, the values that defined sportsmanship, changed? What about so-called private sports clubs? You should have heard the hubbub the night I aired my views about Tiger Woods and the Augusta Golf Club (but like I said, we'll get to that later).

GOOD OLD-FASHIONED LOYALTY, AND WHY PACKERS FANS ARE STILL IN THE GAME

When I grew up, you had your team, and that never changed. No one could make you change your colors any more than someone could make you change your favorite song. Today, people in LA are decked out in Chicago Bulls shirts, while people in Chicago sport Miami Dolphins jerseys. When I grew up, if you wore a "foreign" team color, you were a traitor and risked ridicule. Frankly, you deserved it. Why were you cheering for someone else?

But these days the game has changed. First, the business of professional sports—with the exception of my beloved Green Bay Packers—is all wrong. Unlike the Packers, professional teams are owned by fat cats who make fast cash, have never played sports themselves, and usually have no connection to the place the team is from. The result is that the community ends up having to cheer for some rich guy's team. Why should some honcho from Outer Mongolia own your home team?

I own one share in the Green Bay Packers. The Packers have been a nonprofit corporation since 1923. A total of 4,748,909 shares are owned by 110,901 nut cases like me. My one share cost $200 and entitles me to nothing but pride, and I have lots of it. There are voting rights, but no dividends are ever paid, the stock cannot appreciate in value, and there are no season ticket privileges. Also, no shareholder can own more than 200,000 shares, a safeguard to ensure that no individual can assume control. The Green Bay Packers will never be owned by the richest person in Wisconsin or anywhere else. Rather, the Packers will remain owned by us—a bunch of us.

Now, this is not some socialist idea. In 1997 the existing 1,940 shareholders voted to allow the Packers to sell one million shares to raise money for capital improvements to the stadium. The response was staggering: Paid orders came in at a rate of 3,500 a day, generating $700,000 each day. It's capitalism in all its glory, and no one will leave the stadium unhappy.

And you know what? I would have paid even more for the pride I feel for my team. Look, there's Brett Favre, and Tyrone Williams, and Big Boy Gilbert Brown (go, Gilbert!). These are my guys! I'm invested and devoted, and you can bet I'll let loose with the loudest whoop in the stands (or at least from my couch in Washington, D.C.).

When I turn on the TV and see the green and gold charge out on the field—*my guys*—I feel a connection to the community. I look into the stands and see all my goofy co-owners in below-zero weather with foam cheese wedges on their heads, and my heart swells and I think, *I wish I were there . . . go, Pack!*

Then the cameras scan the owner's box of the competing team and I see bigwigs and fancy clothes, but none of the all-out fun. I actually feel sorry for them. They don't get it. And worse, I feel sorry for their team's fans, because I think they're being cheated. They should own their team, like we do, and experience the pride and the feeling of community.

Second, what is with the stadiums becoming nothing but corporate advertisements? FedExField? The St. Pete Times Forum? The Staples Center? This represents another step away from community, away from individual people who care about the game.

Green Bay's stadium is called Lambeau Field, named after Curly Lambeau, an owner from 1922. That's what it was when I grew up, and that's what it still is. It is not Enron Field, RCA Dome, WorldCom Field, or Merck Coliseum. And, I assure you, Curley Lambeau will never declare bankruptcy, and will never succumb to sleight-of-hand accounting.

LOYAL FANS AND BROKEN HEARTS

Money has poisoned the spirit of many teams. Owners look for better deals and are quick to relocate a team if it can make another buck. The most despicable act is—and I confess my views may be colored by my Baltimore-born-and-raised husband's rant—what happened to the Baltimore Colts. The then-owner of the Colts decided in March 1984 to leave Baltimore and flee to Indianapolis. The move happened—I kid you not—in the middle of a stormy night. A fleet of Mayflower moving vans was pho-tographed leaving the city.

It broke many hearts in Baltimore, a working-class city whose pride was invested in its team. And all for cash, with no regard for loyalty! The owner got to be a big shot in his new digs, while all those fans who had once cheered Johnny Unitas in Memorial Stadium were grief-stricken.

Of course, owners have to make money—and believe me, I have nothing against making money. But a creative person, with that much devotion behind his team, could have come up with a better and more lucrative solution than sneaking out in the mid-dle of the night. What would have been wrong with trying to sell the team to the community? Or, at the very least, leave the old jerseys behind, as well as the team name.

My guess is that there are a lot of other nuts out there like us Packers owners who would be thrilled to spend a few hundred bucks to become co-owners of their favorite team, to literally invest in it and reap the kind of returns that just can't be bought. Old-fashioned loyalty makes sports fun, and full of life.

Money has also poisoned the spirit of many team players. A lot of players seem to have sold out, forgotten what's fundamental to the game. They're a bit too interested in their salaries. I think everyone should get paid what he is worth, but when you make heaps of money, is switching teams for one more shovelful really worth it? When you're making $8 million a year, does it really improve your life so much to make $9 million? I find that inde-fensible. Isn't it more fun, doesn't it enrich your life, to show loy-alty, to play with the devotion and spirit of fans behind you?

Owners need to show loyalty back to the players by making

sure that the players get a salary comparable to what another team might pay. You can't prey on someone's loyalty and not make a fair and just offer.

Loyalty is also required by the community toward the team and the players. The loyalty the Packer fans feel toward the players is unequaled anyplace, even to the point of fanaticism. Frankly, when I was growing up I always wondered: If a Packer player were caught on videotape committing a crime, would there be a juror in the community who would vote to convict him?

I remember one time in the not-so-distant past when a Packer was picked up for a violent crime—sexual assault. My mother, who was then in her eighties—and before hearing any evidence—announced that she thought he'd been framed. I am all for loyalty, but I told my mother that she had gone too far on this one. "Mother, this case is going to court. In sports you pick a side before the game even starts. In a courtroom you pick a side after you hear the facts." I'm thankful my mother wasn't called for jury service on this case.

DOES PLAYING BY THE RULES REQUIRE YOU TO BE FAIR?

Covering sports on a news show is great because we get to talk about issues like corporate ownership. But sports also raise other important issues and allow us to debate about them in a way that feels sometimes safer than debates about politics or religion.

How often in our national conversation do we hear real talk about fairness? What an old-fashioned idea! It's a great issue that is never sufficiently debated, not to mention never resolved.

Where better to have important issues of fairness arise than with sports? We get to cloak the debate with all the niceties and metaphors of sports while we dagger each other with our personal opinions. It somehow seems gentler that way. It can be a safe and spirited debate without getting ugly.

Well, remember when I mentioned golf and Tiger Woods? Whoa, was that a day at *On the Record*! I did a show about the ban on women members at the Augusta National Golf Club back in July 2002. I interviewed two women, one of them the editor of *Golf for Women* magazine, the other an anchor for the Golf Channel. Both thought Augusta should admit women members, but neither was willing to criticize Tiger Woods or pressure him to make a statement in support of admitting women.

Here's the big statement that got me in trouble: "Are you outraged? I'm outraged about two things. One is that we continue to have clubs that won't admit women that have major golf tournaments, and number two, Tiger Woods, who won't stand up for women and say, 'Let the women be members.' "

Boy, did I get e-mails! People seemed to think I was attacking Tiger Woods. I wasn't. Here is one that is printable:

To: ontherecord@foxnews.com
From: Bob in Scottsdale, Arizona

Dear Greta, I have six sisters. I love them dearly. I'm all for women's rights. But c'mon, Tiger should not have to deal with a women's rights issue while he's making the greatest run in golf history. Please, let him focus! Is there really such a dire need for women to be at that golf club? If the women are that desperate, let them build their own golf course down the street. You're making it sound like a little spoiled brat kid that wants what the kid next door has. Yes, I agree, an "only men's" club is not hip these days, but please, leave Tiger alone. He's one of the good eggs. Still love your show.

Bob—you are right, Tiger does not have to do this. I would think he would want to do it. P.S.: With six sisters, you must have had a busy house growing up!

I still think this is a troubling issue that should have everyone aghast. But it's not just about Augusta. There are hundreds of private clubs all over the United States. For years activists in California have been protesting about race and sex discrimination at the Bohemian Club, an elite men's club that each summer hosts a frolic for America's leaders in the redwoods of Sonoma County. There are other fancy country clubs in most states.

In 2001 the Illinois Department of Human Rights found that the Johnson Community Club in Chicago discriminated against women after two women were turned down for membership in the all-male club.

Susan Slavin, a civil rights lawyer and partner in a Long Island, New York, law firm, told the *New York Times* on August 5, 2001, that many golf clubs in her area discriminate against women. The Huntington Crescent Club, she said, admits women only if they are daughters of current members.

Now, the National Golf Foundation claims that six million women are playing golf. Doesn't discrimination at golf clubs just sound plain stupid? Second—and this I do not get—why would someone want to discriminate? What's the big thrill with that?

Should women be admitted to membership at Augusta or not? The cloak here is golf, but the dagger is a fundamental issue of fairness. Is it fair to require men to admit women to their clubs? Is it fair to exclude women when so many business deals are made in clubs and so many public activities are held there? Is it fair to demand that Tiger Woods stand up and support women? Especially when you consider the fact that until the early '90s, the club refused membership to African Americans.

The law is clear—an entirely private club can exclude women. The question is, when does a private club transform its nature and become not entirely private? If a club accepts tax breaks or public money, I say it is not private. When it transforms itself into a "public accommodation," it is no longer private. That line of transformation—the "public accommodation" line—is yet to be defined by the Supreme Court in the case of Augusta National, but my guess is that someday soon the Court will do so.

But the real matter is way beyond what the law may require. It is the social question. Do we really want to be a society that excludes people because of gender? Does that make us proud? Do you not want your mother, sister, or daughter to have a chance to do what a man can do if she is equally able? Look at how women's ability has changed as the doors have opened for women in sports, just for example.

As much as we try to make this great country the fairest place on earth—and it is—it's not perfect. We need to work on a few things. Sometimes it's the little things that we overlook. Something that may not seem important to you may have enormous importance to others. (I, for example, really couldn't care less about golf membership for me. I don't play golf. I don't *want* to play golf. If you wanted to torture me, you could sentence me to a few hours lolling around on a green in plaid Bermuda shorts. I just don't get it. Never have, and probably never will. And more importantly, I think it is a public service that I do not play golf. I have a sneaking suspicion I would badly hack up the course with my lack of skill.) But denying opportunity to others may be the worst social crime we can inflict on each other. "Give everybody a chance!" is about as close as you can come to our national slogan.

Sometimes oppression is so covert, so much a part of the social fabric, that people just don't recognize it. No one gets it. And that's harmful to everyone. Somebody who is keeping someone else, or a whole group of someone elses, down and doesn't even see it is also hurt by the injustice. Aren't our lives less full, less fun, when we're restricted by our fears or the habits we've grown comfortable inside of?

Maybe some men, like Hootie Johnson, chairman of Augusta National, don't even see the problem. Maybe Johnson doesn't see how his club's exclusions harm women. He's the kind of guy who would point to the fact that since there is one woman CEO of a Fortune 500 company, that means there is no lingering discrimination in corporate America. "See?" Hootie would say. "*That* woman is there, so there's no problem."

It can't be ignored that August National is a place where many business contacts are made. CEOs of major companies are members of this club. Warren Buffett of Berkshire Hathaway, Sanford

Weill of Citicorp, and Kenneth Chenault of American Express, along with Bill Gates of Microsoft, are all members. To deny women membership is to deny them the opportunities that come with rubbing shoulders with influential corporate executives.

Is the all-male decision to exclude women from membership at Augusta covert or overt oppression? Are women being denied an opportunity to be big players in the business world?

Frankly, I don't get why a club would want to exclude women. But here's the rub: If Augusta is truly private, than I believe it has a right to exclude women. People in this country have a right to many things, including the right to be rude in many instances. I defend those rights. I have defended lots of jerks in my life in the name of the Constitution, and I can't see being inconsistent here. I would not like to defend Augusta, but if Augusta is truly private, I would defend its right to exclude women.

But we all know what private means. You don't televise tournaments to a national audience from a private club. You don't let nonmembers in. You want to be private, fine. But be private, then! No public benefits, perks, or publicity. Private means private.

However, if indeed Augusta National is truly private—a question yet to be resolved by the Supreme Court—wouldn't it be better and more honorable for them to say, "We are private and we do not have to admit women to membership. However, in recognition of the importance of the business community and the recognition that women are part of that community, we believe the right thing to do is admit women"?

Take the Bohemian Club, that San Francisco institution that holds what President Herbert Hoover once called "the greatest men's party on earth." That party has been held since 1879 at the

2,700-acre Bohemian Grove in Monte Rio, about 70 miles north of San Francisco in Sonoma County. In 1999 participants were reported to include former President George Bush as well as his son, Henry Kissinger, Colin Powell, former House Speaker Newt Gingrich, and Dow Chemical chairman Frank Popoff.

Journalists are barred—now that I can understand—but *so are women*. The problem is that the guys get to hear things like Colin Powell giving a talk called "America's Promise: Leading Armies and Leading Kids" and Frank Popoff giving a speech called "Environmental Journey." Shouldn't some women at least have a chance to join the fray and listen in?

I love it when people stand up and do the right thing, not because they have to but because they know *it is the right thing to do*. I love someone who has conviction. Remember Martin Luther King Jr. and his dream? Ronald Reagan on communism, when he told Gorbachev to tear down the Berlin Wall? How can you not love greatness?

As for Tiger Woods . . . he does not have to stake out the position that he will refuse to play where women are not yet members. The law does not require him to take that position. The law does not demand that people take the high moral ground. The law does not require that, given the opportunity, one must do the right thing and speak out for those who are unable to do so. But something else *does* require that of all of us, and that is a call to fairness.

Every time Tiger Woods is asked about Augusta, many people wonder, "How could a man who himself has been discriminated against—by this very club, for only bad reasons—not understand and take action?"

Many wish that Tiger Woods would step up to the plate and

force the issue because, quite simply, he can. By virtue of his immense talent, he has the respect and admiration of so many. People would listen to him. Well, I for one wish he would speak up. I like to see a great man become greater, and by speaking out, I believe, he would.

COMPETITIVE CARS AND RATINGS-DRIVEN NEWS ANCHORS

When I first started covering NASCAR on my show, I got a fair amount of flak from viewers and friends. What's a serious news show doing covering auto racing?

On a show about NASCAR, I was chatting with several of Fox's sports reporters. We noted that millions of people are now watching NASCAR on television, that the sport has taken on respectability. Jeff Gordon hosted *Saturday Night Live,* not exactly a redneck TV show. But we also noted that some of the recent tabloid-type stuff has increased interest in the sport. Here is part of our conversation:

Greta: Until recently I didn't pay much attention to NASCAR until I started hearing about Tony Stewart and Jeff Gordon, and I started doing segments on it. I now find myself watching it. It's almost, it's a little bit of an addictive sport. It really is getting more popular, at least it seems that way.

Rob Becker, Fox Sports: Well that's the soap opera, big star effect, and Greta, you really symbolize this country because you've gotten more into it because of the personalities. I don't think you've gotten more into it because of the race car strategy, have you?

Greta: Well, not particularly, because I don't fully understand the race car strategy. Maybe you could explain. I mean, when I watch it, though, what do I want to look for? I mean, what is it that's so intriguing? I mean, I look for the winner, but I assume there's a strategy to get there.

Becker: Well, you know, the pit stops, when you take the pit stop, when you're running out of gas, when you've got to change your tires, that's the strategy. I wouldn't say that's as much strategy as you find in a pro football game, but there is some. But in the end, you still are going to pay attention, I assume even if you don't really get into when exactly someone takes their pit stop.

Greta: Well, I'm trying to pay attention. I'm trying to learn. Dave Van Dyck, what is it about NASCAR that captures you? What do you think is fun about it?

Dave Van Dyck, FoxSports.com: You know, Greta, you're a typical fan. What happens is you tune in and you say I'm rooting for Jeff Gordon or Kevin Harvick or Dale Earnhardt Jr., somebody. And what happens is, you get a weekly soap opera.

Am I proud that I started paying attention because Jeff Gordon's divorce proceedings showed him to be worth $48 million and to be netting over $1 million a month after taxes? No. But I'm human, and my eyeballs got wide when I realized that a NASCAR champion could make that kind of money. This sport must really have grown! Why? I was curious about why the stands are packed with avid, screaming fans—and then I got hooked!

So did a lot of other people. The television ratings for NASCAR broadcasts have far exceeded expectations. Ken Schanzer, president of NBC Sports, which shares the NASCAR contract with Fox, Turner, and FX, said in December 2002 that ratings were up 59 percent over two years. Over fifteen million people watch NASCAR. It's loud, it's fast, it's death-defying! I have had the thrill of interviewing Winston Cup champion Tony Stewart and learned so much. Did you know that each track has its own "personality," which a driver must know intimately in order to win? NASCAR gets my adrenaline going and has me screaming from my perch on the couch, "Go, Tony!" And while we're at it, I'll be rooting for Leilani Munter and Shawna Robinson. Who says women can't drive?

Whether it's NASCAR or golf or track, sports are often the first time we learn about competition and fairness, and that's why they're important. And let me say one last thing about sports figures as role models. When I was growing up in Appleton, the heroes in our state were Green Bay Packers players. Beginning when I was about seven, my father used to take me every Monday night to Fuzzy's Left Guard, Fuzzy Thurston's restaurant, which is today called Fuzzy's Shenanigans. (For those of you who somehow might not know this, Fuzzy was a former left guard and a legendary Hall of Famer.) That was the night Vince Lombardi gave the players off, and the restaurant would be filled with the team.

They were such great men. They would hoist me up on their shoulders and give me rides around the place! They were sweet and gentle and fun. They were my role models. They were my heroes.

11

GETTING RICH THROUGH FAILURE OR FRAUD

Executives should be rewarded for success, not failure. Big corporations need to be responsible and treat workers and investors with honesty and respect. That is real patriotism.

For me it's not a big leap from fairness in sports to fairness in the workplace. The same rules of conduct apply no matter what the game.

A few years ago I was interviewing Ted Turner, the founder of CNN and, at the time, one of the world's richest businessmen. This wasn't long after he had pledged $1 billion to the United Nations, and I want to share with you something he told me. I asked him why he was giving away so much money. He turned to me and said that $100 million was a "saturation point."

"Once you have $100 million, you don't need any more, Greta. There is nothing in life you can't do with $100 million. Having $200 million won't change your life from having $100 million."

I've thought about that a lot as I have watched corporate greed and irresponsibility devastate the stock market and wipe out people's retirement accounts. How much money does anybody need? And at what price to others?

APPLETON, WISCONSIN . . . AGAIN

I know, I know, you're thinking, *Here we go again as she tells us how great everything was back in a small midwestern city in 1950–70s.*

Hang on. It wasn't perfect. Lots of families in my town worked for the Kimberly-Clark Corporation. In fact, they were employed by that company their whole lives. I thought working for a big corporation like that might be boring. But it did provide security for families. Grandfathers, fathers, sons, uncles worked for the company. The company was family. The employees were proud of the company and the management was proud of employees. Over time, many would come to think that if you worked for the company until you were sixty-five you would get a pension you could live on. Forget that! There are no more pensions, just 401(k) plans that only permit you to put your money into the stock market. Maybe you don't want to do that; maybe you don't want to play the market. But in today's corporation you have no choice.

Let me tell you what else worked back then. Smallness. In my town there were lots of small businesses: retail stores, banks, real estate offices, movie theaters. They were all owned by actual people who lived in the community, who raised their kids there. It created a sense of responsibility for everyone because every time you conducted business you were doing so with your neighbor. Nobody could get away with cooking the books, and nobody could destroy his business and then leave with a golden parachute. Anyone who did that would have been run out of town. Businesspeople felt a responsibility to be accountable to their community. Am I being too nostalgic about American business in the 1950s and 1960s? Well, maybe. But I'll tell you one thing I am pretty sure about: The companies and businesses in those days were not stealing from their employees, defrauding investors, or treating employees like criminals or animals. And CEOs were not making $100 million annual salaries. In the old days CEOs focused on making sure the revenues exceeded the expenses. They also took great pride in watching their employees thrive.

I never worked for a big corporation before I joined CNN. I just never thought I'd fit in at a huge company with thousands of employees. I always thought I'd want to work at a smaller place, a place that could be more personal, where you felt responsibility for the company's successes and failures. I also felt I would like to be my own boss. In fact, when I joined CNN, I thought it was a mom-and-pop operation. I knew who ran it and I referred to them by their first names, and I wasn't alone in this. It may have had a huge global reach, but in terms of its corporate culture, CNN seemed to me a mom-and-pop operation in the early years.

But whether an organization is large or small, the question is the same: For whom does the company work? Does it work for the employees and its customers, or does it work for Wall Street?

It seems that just about everyone wants to get rich, and I don't think there's anything wrong with that . . . unless you got there by being a criminal or by excelling at failure. Get rich fairly and never forget for whom you work. Get rich by being innovative and industrious. That's the old-fashioned way.

The employee's job is to do his best work for the company. The company's job is to conduct itself with integrity, make its products work well and safely for the consumer, and treat its employees fairly. The company does *not* work for Wall Street! If it maintains its responsibility to its first two missions—treating customers and employees right—it should grow and prosper, and its stock will be valued appropriately and not inflated. Investors may not get rich overnight. But guess what? They are not supposed to. It doesn't hurt to be patient and get rich over time, rather than overnight.

SYNERGY

In the "new days," CEOs have MBAs and talk about "synergy." I run when I hear that term. Synergy is the big idea, the one that is supposed to propel American business to new heights. Henry Ford had an engine. Remember Bob Pittman, the deposed AOL Time Warner leader? He promoted synergy. Let me tell you why I think folks like Pittman and the synergy crowd are, in most cases, empty suits.

When Time Inc., an old magazine company, merged with Warner Brothers, a newer but well-established entertainment company, there was this idea that each could contribute to the other's business. (Back in the 1990s they were also calling it "convergence.") It wasn't an immediately successful marriage. The Warner folks were hipsters and had trendy haircuts; the Time people were buttoned-down nerds. The corporate cultures of these two companies were as different as they could possibly be. Some people joked that Time was so WASPish and Warner so Jewish that the company holidays would have to be doubled. But slowly the two organizations were brought together in an uneasy but profitable partnership, encouraged mostly by the charm and determination of Warner chief Steve Ross. What was most important was that each side had a great product: Warner had a deep library of movies and records, and Time had an unmatched stable of magazines. Separately, these businesses were profitable.

Then in 1995 Time and Turner Broadcasting, which owned CNN, merged. And they started to talk synergy. Gerald Levin and the deal makers referred to Time's magazines and CNN's broadcasting as two solid journalistic "brands." Huh? Is that like deodorant or laundry soap? Nobody was sure what it meant. Was it all about advertising? Would advertisers be able to buy a page in *Time* and a minute on CNN? Or would the staffs work together? Nobody seemed to have a clue.

The urgency of the merger was fueled by the Internet. It was as though a fever of greed overtook the media companies, who suddenly believed they had to match up with the Internet or die. A rush of shotgun marriages was proposed. But by 2001 this idea of media companies building branded Web sites had become a disaster. Disney lost its shirt with Go.com, and NBC's Snap.com failed miserably.

Barry Meyer, chairman of the Warner Brothers movie and television studio, said something interesting recently: "I don't think synergy as concept is dead, but it has to arise viscerally—come from a need rather than being imposed." Barry Meyer was right.

Television and print are different, even if they are both journalism. How would Time and CNN be synergistic? One cynical *Time* magazine reporter at the time summed up the intent of the merger by wisecracking, "Synergy? It means they're gonna strap cameras on our heads and try to save money." She wasn't far from wrong. The first big "synergy" between Time and CNN was a "joint investigation" of O.J. Simpson's finances during the civil trial in 1997. So what did that mean? It meant that *Time*'s investigative reporters uncovered the sources of Simpson's money and CNN ran round-the-clock broadcasts of the magazine's story, touting it a joint "*Time*-CNN investigation." The story inside the magazine carried the banner "*Time*-CNN investigation." It was nothing of the sort, and most good journalists inside both organizations knew it. CNN was brilliant at breaking news but had never devoted big resources to investigation. *Time* was a weekly in an age of instant news and wasn't specializing in breaking stories. Still, the bean counters and executives wanted to make it look like—aha!—synergy was working. It was a joke.

Then came the AOL Time Warner merger, and synergy was an even greater imperative for one reason: This deal was *huge,* the largest merger in history. The fact that a start-up information conduit company like AOL, which many people even then thought had an inflated value for a company that actually manufactured nothing, could swallow up a company like Time Warner, which if nothing else actually produced stuff, seemed bizarre and outrageous to many of us. But it was all about synergy.

What the hell were they thinking? Here is the best I can figure, and we'll use Madonna as an example of what synergy might have been for AOL Time Warner.

Ready?

Madonna makes a record for her company that is owned by Warner Records. She gets free or discounted advertising on CNN, HBO, and TNT, to use some TV examples; she gets free ads in *People, Time, Sports Illustrated,* and a bunch of other magazines owned by the company. Then all those magazines do positive cover stories about Madonna and the record. *Time* covers it as "Madonna—What Does She Represent to American Women?" *People's* cover says, "Madonna—Will Her Marriage Survive Another Success?" *Fortune's* cover is "Madonna—Behind the Slick Business Empire." You get the idea. Warner Books decides to publish her authorized biography. Then the Warner Brothers movie studio signs Madonna to star in a picture, uses her music for the soundtrack, and gets ready to promote the concert tour, which sells out immediately.

But wait! There are a number of great seats available only to AOL subscribers. The brilliant business theory, then, is that 86,422,567 people, from brewmeisters in Hanover, Germany, to fishermen in Togo, will say, "Whoa! I better sign up for AOL as my Internet service provider so I can get to see Madonna when she plays here at the Togo stadium!"

Now, there are a few problems here. First, AOL's Bob Pittman seemed to think the sky was the limit with this great idea, and he promised everything to everybody. He didn't seem to have a clue that those magazines actually consider themselves part of journalism. You can't exactly tell a reporter that he has to do a puff piece about Madonna because "we're all in the same business here." Well, you can try, but you're going to get big-time resistance.

Madonna *did* do a concert tour that included special tickets for AOL members. But guess what? It sure didn't result in the spike of members they predicted and had promised Wall Street.

Time Warner was already stressed on the synergy business even as the AOL takeover was being hatched. *Time* editor in chief Norman Pearlstein told the *Wall Street Journal* that before they went to press he read every story in every Time Inc. magazine that made any mention of a company owned by Time Warner to make sure "it was fair." He seemed proud of that. Huh? He didn't read all the stories in the magazines, just those that mentioned HBO or the Warner Brothers studios? Didn't he realize how that made reporters feel? One journalist said, "Norman Pearlstein doesn't have anything better to do than copyedit my story at midnight on Friday, taking out a negative reference to Warner? That's called a chilling effect." I don't know Norman Pearlstein, but I know what some in the company thought about the merger of Time and Warner Brothers.

Bottom line (and I think you probably guessed it already): I am *not* a fan of synergy. It's impossible to predict whether the idea will ever really be useful. Better business minds than mine will have their predictions. But I *can* speak to common sense and say: Don't try to force synergy and other harebrained schemes on companies that were doing just fine before.

STOCK OPTIONS—ANOTHER THING THAT MAKES ME NUTS

During round one of my contract negotiation with CNN, they offered me stock options. In addition to my proposed salary, in their first offer they offered me 25,000 shares. At the time the stock was at about $27 per share, and they told me that the value of those 25,000 options was between $250,000 and $300,000. They also said the stock was going to shoot to $60 a share. Read on.

My husband, John, and I sat down and looked at this. I

thought CNN—which by that time was owned by AOL—was going down the drain. I thought the management was messing up everything. I knew what they were doing to morale, and I know the value of morale to profit. So how could they be so sure that I was going to make money at $27 a share?

It didn't make sense to me. I vaguely remember them saying there was a formula for valuations, something with a name like "black book" (which made me instantly think of the *Kelley Blue Book*, which values used cars). As it turns out, there is no simple blue book for valuing stock options, but at the time I thought there must be.

Anyway, it just didn't make sense to me. The promise of future stock options in a company that I didn't think was doing so well seemed vague. I told them I couldn't for the life of me figure out how the darn things were valued. And so I said I'd pass on the stock options and think about a better salary instead.

So what did they do? They offered me more options! Go figure! The whole thing began to feel like a magic trick. At the time stock options were the hot item in corporate America. High-salaried employees and dot-com types grabbed them when they were offered, and companies were handing them out like candy.

I said, "No, thanks—it seems like funny money to me."

Boy, was that a smart decision.

Let me tell you what this stock option business is really all about. I've only mastered this recently, and it sure wasn't easy to understand. No wonder companies have been able to get so much mileage out of offering options without a revolt.

Stock options are a relatively new thing for employees. Essentially the idea is that the option gives an employee the right to buy shares in his company at a fixed price for a certain number of years. The price at which the option is given is called the grant price and is usually the market price at the time the option is given. The idea is that the stock price will go up, and employees can buy the stock at the lower price and sell it at the higher one.

In 1992 about 1 million employees had stock options. By 2002 that had grown to nearly 10 million people. Senior executives get the lion's share, but more and more mainstream companies (General Electric, PepsiCo, Coca-Cola, Bank of America, and Merck, for example) offer broad-based plans to all employees. In general, the idea isn't a bad one: The employees get a stake in their company's growth and are invested in its long-term success—assuming it's a healthy company that's not playing accounting games.

But stock options cost companies money, and the question is whether the corporation is fully disclosing to its shareholders how much they cost. U.S. accounting rule makers are considering forcing companies to disclose stock option expenses on their income statements. In other words, let investors know all the facts. And do it in a way that they can understand without first getting an MBA or becoming a CPA.

Some companies—General Electric, Coca-Cola, and General Motors—have already agreed to count options as an expense. In my opinion they get high marks for doing so, and for making full disclosure so that investors don't run the risk of being misled. Others, such as Intel, Microsoft, and Cisco Systems, are refusing to do it, arguing that they can't find the right formula to value them.

Wait a minute. CNN had no problem telling me valuations—

remember, my 25,000 shares were ostensibly, according to them, worth between $250,000 and $300,000. So what's going on? It turns out the "black book" thing CNN was talking about was this obscure method called the Black-Scholes formula. That was how AOL Time Warner was valuing options. Even the editors of the *Wall Street Journal* recently confessed they didn't thoroughly understand it. It is, in short, a complex formula based largely on dividend yields and volatility. (Okay, I confess: I barely understand yields and volatility. How about you?)

In July 2002 *Business Week* magazine studied the bottom-line impact of different methods of valuing options. Of Black-Scholes, CNN's method, *Business Week* said one of its disadvantages was that it "overestimates option value."

You bet it does. "Overestimates option value" is a polite business-school description of what AOL was so "generously" offering me. Frankly, I knew I was being hoodwinked, and I was a bit surprised that after all these years they thought I was that naive.

Three other methods got a thumbs-down. But then *Business Week* found a method that works, and guess what it's called: "intrinsic value." What a concept! The value of an option is the stock price minus the exercise price. That gives you its value. Since on the grant date the value is zero, fixed accounting can't be used. *Business Week* said, "This method accurately tracks the true options value over time. Uses no 'assumptions' that can be tweaked to boost earnings."

Why does this matter? Not because high-salaried employees like myself who are presumably smart enough to figure this stuff out could be misled—no one should feel sorry for us—but because the average guy has been forgotten by Wall Street. Large corporations rule those pension funds and rule his future. The stock option fiasco that devastated those funds has devastated average employees.

My take: Force companies to expense options based on intrinsic value. It simply requires them to be open. Full and simple disclosure is a good idea, and it is the right thing to do.

And if they don't? If a CEO says it's too hard to figure out, well, find one who can. If you are smart enough to be a CEO and run a public company, you'd better be smart enough to figure out how to give full disclosure.

AND NOW, ON TO GREED

Addressing the criminal aspect of failing corporations is actually quite easy. We all know what stealing is. We all know what fraud is. And we have plenty of laws that can be utilized to punish criminals. The more difficult issue is morality. How do you get people to be decent? You can't pass a law that demands decency. No one is perfect, but you have to wonder what it is that turned so many corporate chiefs into heartless criminals. And when I think about this I'm reminded of my days as a criminal lawyer, because there's an aspect of these corporate transgressions that seems pretty close to the psychology of the average criminal. I don't think anyone becomes a criminal overnight—it takes time. You stretch the rules a bit here and no one notices, so you stretch a bit more over there. Repetition starts to dull the sense of wrongdoing. And it just gets easier as you go along.

Think about the serial armed robber. I had a lot of cases like this when I practiced criminal law. The defendant would tell me that the first time he held someone up at gunpoint it was enormously stressful. He was incredibly nervous—would sweat, even feel guilty. Often first-timers find the robbery itself terrifying and wrong. But after a few more stickups, he managed to convince himself that not only was it easy, but he was right. He deserved that money or that television set. He had an easy time justifying it. I think that's what some of these corporate executives accused of fancy accounting did. Somehow they got accustomed to it, and they justified it to themselves. It became easy, and over time any hint of possible indecency simply vanished from their consciousness. It's the old "everybody does it, so it must be right" excuse. You have heard the phrase "That's the way it is done" used to justify its rightness.

Too many companies are playing footloose and fancy free with accounting practices and then feigning ignorance. What is footloose accounting? Here is what I mean. Let's go to Dennis Kozlowski's $18 million apartment in Manhattan. The fact is that for all the criticism he and Tyco received for this art-filled pad that Tyco owned but Dennis lived in, the arrangement was not unusual. General Electric owns four apartments in luxury buildings in New York. The company doesn't disclose the apartments in government filings because "it hasn't been required," according to spokesman Gary Sheffer.

Last year GE bought a $11.3 million apartment for the use of its chairman and CEO, Jeffrey Immelt. Another apartment is used by NBC chairman Robert Wright, and another was for the lifetime use of former GE chairman Jack Welch. Sheffer said he didn't know whether these executives declare the value of the apartments on their income taxes. Well, shouldn't he? Particularly in the wake of the devastating scandal over Welch's postretirement compensation package? Disclosure may not be legally required, but if I were a shareholder, I sure would want to know how much the company I had invested in was shelling out for the care and feeding of its present and former chief executives.

And the list goes on. PepsiCo owns two apartments in Manhattan. Rayovac bought a home in Westport, Wisconsin, for its chairman and CEO, David Jones, as part of his compensation package. A Rayovac spokesman wouldn't tell the *Wall Street Journal* what the home cost, but its assessed value was $832,200, according to public records. I am from Wisconsin and I can tell you that you can buy a magnificent home for $832,200. Wisconsin is not Manhattan.

If they are not giving their CEOs homes, too many companies simply give them multimillion-dollar loans that often have clauses allowing the loans to be forgiven if the executive stays at the company a few years.

How does that sound when you imagine walking into a bank and trying to get a loan even when you've been a loyal employee of a company for ten years? Is the company helping you get a mortgage? In an environment of creative bookkeeping, these practices become part of the corporate culture and become, in the minds of its senior executives, morally acceptable. At least this is my theory for how so many execs can day after day play with and massage the numbers—and cause so much hurt to so many people. It just starts to feel normal to them.

I say let's have a "separation of church and state" in publicly held companies. Any executive expenses related to home, play, or personal travel are exactly that, *personal,* meaning executives should pay for them out of their own salary. The company and its employees and investors should not pay for them!

CEOs WHO BUY $6,000 SHOWER CURTAINS WITH COMPANY FUNDS, AND OTHER SWEET TALES

I want to talk to you about companies like Enron, but also about what has happened in a number of other corporations. Enron was just the tip of the iceberg, but it has become the quintessential example of corporate abuse and malfeasance, and the effects of the Enron scandal will be felt for years and years. In 1999 Enron was ranked in the top ten on the Fortune 500 list of big U.S. companies, and Wall Street loved it, sending the stock price to a high of $90 a share. When Enron declared bankruptcy in December 2001, they revealed that, yes, they had overstated their profits to the tune of $600 million since 1997. And oh, yes, they hid debt in secret off-book partnerships run by their own officers.

The American companies that have been found to have cooked the books, or are suspected of doing so, are almost too many to list. Even the Securities and Exchange Commission can't keep up. WorldCom, Rite Aid, Anderson, Tyco, Merck . . . Unfortunately this business of corporate shenanigans has hit everybody. The University of Michigan's Health and Retirement Study found in July 2002 that about $678 billion of retirees' savings has been wiped out during the last two years. That is an awful lot of money for those people who invested in the stock market—

people who invested and believed in American business and the people who lead it.

Let me digress here to say that my personal hero in business is Warren Buffett, and I dearly wish that more CEOs would adopt his leadership ideals. If you'd put $10,000 into Berkshire Hathaway when Buffett took control of it in 1965, you'd have more than $50 million today, compared to the just under $500,000 you'd have if you'd invested in the Standard & Poor's 500 stock index.

Buffet is seventy-two, and though he's a billionaire he continues to live on Farnam Street in Omaha, in the same stucco house he bought forty years ago for $31,500. He eats hamburgers for lunch and drinks Coca-Cola—a company in which he has invested since 1988.

In his newsletter to Berkshire Hathaway shareholders in March 2003 and in subsequent speeches Buffet insisted that American business has to earn back the trust of the public. "What really gets the public is when CEOs get very rich and stay very rich and they get very poor," Buffett said.

And who's he talking about? The middle-class Americans who thought that investing in solid American industries, in sound companies that produced automobiles and energy, that developed telecommunications, that conducted research in pharmaceuticals, was a safe and maybe even patriotic thing to do.

Did this have to happen? Are all these losses just the results of a predictable downturn in economic times? Just part of the business cycle?

I say no, and I'll tell you why. I worked for one of these big corporations and I saw how things were done. I was not at all surprised when AOL came under investigation. The business practices of AOL, from their stock valuations to their accounting habits, are a perfect example of what needs to be carefully scrutinized. Something was odd—the company's stock price began falling like a rock, and many shareholders got hurt while a select few seemed to make out extremely well. But before I get to AOL Time Warner, the company that is not in legal trouble (yet), let's look at a few that are and how they got that way. With all due respect to the hardworking federal investigators who are poring over the books, this stuff is not hard to figure out.

Tyco International was an amazing company, making the cover of *Business Week* in 2001 and hailed as a fiercely competitive company hungry for acquisitions and expansions. Tyco was headed by Dennis Kozlowski, who grew up in a poor neighborhood in Newark, New Jersey. Dennis' father was a police detective. Dennis wanted to make good, and he got himself into Seton Hall, a respected Catholic university in New Jersey, where he got an accounting degree. In 1975, soon after graduation, he joined Tyco.

Kozlowski started out in Tyco as a lowly auditor. He worked his way up the ladder, just like we all hope we might. By the time he became CEO in 1992 he was touted as the best of a new breed of aggressive executive. As late as January 2002 *Business Week* named him one of the country's twenty-five best managers. Kozlowski also was one of the nation's highest-paid CEOs, raking in $125 million in salary in 2000, but nobody complained because Tyco was making money for shareholders and was growing by swallowing up other companies. The world was rosy. Or at least that's the way it looked as long as nobody looked too hard. Because a closer look showed that as old Dennis was raking it in, he was also causing pain. Some six thousand workers in Tyco's electronics division were laid off in November 2001. The financial press somehow calls that kind of thing "belt-tightening" without raising an eyebrow about CEO pay.

Somewhere along the way Dennis went even further wrong. I'm reminded of Warren Buffett's recent comment about the rash of CEO misconduct, which he emphasized by quoting a Mae West line: "Once I was Snow White, and then I drifted." Dennis Kozlowski, once the good schoolboy, definitely drifted. I believe he forgot the important things and got caught up in a world of greed and corporate wrongdoing that has begun to pass for normal business practices.

Kozlowski was indicted in June 2002 on sales tax evasion charges. We're not talking small stuff here. He had purchased a few Renoirs and Monets to the tune of $13.8 million and supposedly had them shipped to Tyco's New Hampshire office to avoid paying sales tax. The only problem was that they didn't go to New Hampshire and instead ended up hanging in Dennis' New York apartment, a place that Tyco had purchased with company funds for $18 million.

The poor kid from New Jersey wanted to hobnob in the world of the rich. He bought Rolls-Royces, outfitted a $20,000 Harley Davidson, flew private jets, and bought mansions in Boca Raton, Florida. He sailed around in his 130-foot boat, *Endeavor,* according to prosecutors. The only thing Dennis didn't seem to want to do was to pay his fair share of taxes. If the charges are true, it seems like he felt that everyone, including the employees and shareholders of Tyco, owed him.

I don't think there's anything wrong with trying to get rich, nor with living it up if you're lucky enough to have made it. I do have a problem if the shareholders and employees are paying for all your stuff without their knowledge. We don't know yet who paid for those paintings and some of the other toys. But if Tyco employees and shareholders paid for them, didn't know it, and didn't agree to it, then something is terribly wrong.

Now get this: Even though Kozlowski resigned under a cloud, as the financial press puts it, using a rather quaint euphemism for indictment, he still negotiated to keep his severance under the retention agreement that would have kicked in if he had been fired. That retention agreement provided for $135 million, plus $3.4 million annually for a thirty-day-a-year consulting contract for the rest of his life.

Meanwhile, Tyco lost $80 billion—yes, *billion*—in market value. The stock went from $60 a share to about $14 as this book went to press.

But back to Dennis' severance deal. If you think it's surprising and that Dennis was particularly clever to have negotiated this rich parting gift for himself, you are quite wrong. Almost every one of the top executives at the most disgraced companies in America has walked away with a lucrative pay package. It's just part of corporate life in America. My favorite golden-parachute story concerns the platinum corporate boot that Michael Ovitz got from Disney. It's generally agreed that Ovitz failed during his tenure as the number two man at Disney. He and chairman Michael Eisner just didn't see eye to eye. So he was pushed out the door, according to reports, with about $100 million. This kind of deal is not the exception, it's the rule. And guess who ends up paying for it when the company is publicly traded? The stockholders.

I think we need a refresher course for CEOs. Here goes: You work for the company. That means the employees, customers, and investors. You owe them! They do not owe you.

ANOTHER FAVORITE EXAMPLE

Finally, back to one of my favorite topics: AOL Time Warner. I can't think of a more perfect example of all that is wrong with corporate America and needs fixing now. I've already talked about my career at CNN and why I left, but I think it's also important to put things in a broader perspective.

Since AOL bought Time Warner in January 2000, some eight thousand employees were given the old heave-ho. In some ways they were the lucky ones, because the ninety thousand workers left have watched their 401(k) accounts plummet as AOL stock has gone from $60 to about $13 a share. During the merger, all those Time Warner employees were forced to give up their profit-sharing plans for stock options. What are those options worth now? Zip.

There is real pain there. People's savings were decimated, and for those in their forties and fifties, people who were planning retirement in the relatively near future, the loss was devastating.

The AOL Time Warner merger buried the company in debt; earlier this year the company wrote down nearly $100 billion of assets, a stunning devaluation of the company and the largest in corporate history. High-priced financial analysts recommended this? Suze Orman could have given them better advice.

So did everyone feel the pain? Not a chance. Gerald Levin, the man who managed what is now considered to be one of the worst mergers in business history, cashed out $153 million worth of stock options in 2000. Didn't he believe that the company was going to do well and prosper? He told his employees and his investors and Wall Street he did. But then why did he bail?

In 2001 Richard Parsons, the current chairman of AOL, did the same thing, earning $27 million on his options. Steve Case, the AOL chief, dumped two million AOL Time Warner shares between February and May 2001, making $100 million.

And Bob Pittman, the former CFO and captain of synergy, sold the stock at a peak price, making $66 million.

So was any of that illegal? No. Immoral? In my opinion, yes. My answer is to tie stock options to performance and don't let executives exercise options until they leave a company. They want to share the wealth? Great! Let 'em share the ride on the way down.

Maybe some corporate leaders are beginning to get it. Citigroup chairman and chief executive officer Sanford Weill recently said he'd forgo a bonus because of a 25 percent decline in the company's share price last year. He got options to buy 1.5 million shares, worth about $14.5 million, the bank said. With 450,000 options received last year, worth $5.8 million, and his $1 million salary, his total compensation last year fell 78 percent from 2001's $30.3 million.

But some others don't get it and are still not taking responsibility. It's not hard to identify the corporate practices that seem blatantly immoral. Take Qwest Communications. Four former executives of the Denver-based telephone company were indicted for accounting fraud in February 2003, and the company was facing a potential bankruptcy court filing.

So is Qwest admitting wrongdoing and paying the price? Nope. As of March 2003 they had spent $75 million hiring eight of the highest-priced law firms in the country to defend themselves. It was estimated that they were spending $7 million a month on lawyers. Qwest says those fees are being paid out of its insurance. But guess what? Eight of its insurers claim the company misled them about the status of its accountants, and they want to rescind $325 million of coverage. If they succeed, shareholders will be left holding the bag for legal fees and settlements.

Or how about the CEO of Sprint Corporation, William Esrey? He is complaining that he got bad legal advice from Ernst and Young, the accounting firm, when it offered him a tax shelter. Now the IRS may rule the shelter illegal. If they do, Esrey will owe $123 million. But who is responsible? Esrey, Ernst and Young, or both?

I confess I am not a fan of Ernst and Young. The giant accounting firms have been a big disappointment to shareholders in this country. They did not protect those who invested their life savings in companies that have now gone belly up or nearly so. But it is also hard for me to feel sorry for Mr. Esrey. In 1998, 1999, and 2000 he exercised stock options that produced profits of $159 million. He would have $63 million in taxes without the shelter.

So how did Sprint employees and shareholders fare while the executives were cashing in options and grabbing tax shelters? In

2002 Sprint cut seventeen thousand jobs. Since reaching a high of $75.50 in November 1999, Sprint shares were hovering near $12 as this book went to press in March 2003.

CEOs and top management are treated differently than everybody else who works for the company. I don't disagree with this as long as the CEO and top management are acting responsibly toward the company employees and the shareholders and the company is profitable. In other words, the CEO and top management must earn it and not be unjustly rewarded for failure or indecency.

You might find it interesting to know that in 2002 some CEOs made 411 times as much as the average factory worker. That statistic surprised me. How should compensation be determined? Common sense plus a fundamental commitment to fairness—to employees, customers, business partners, and stockholders—ought to lead any intelligent corporate CEO and board of directors to the right and true answer.

HERE'S WHAT THE VIEWERS SAID

As the business scandals of the past year or two mushroomed—Martha Stewart, Tyco, Enron, and so on—people really began to feel the pain and to understand what was going on. Here's an example from my show. At the beginning of this corporate meltdown, and several times subsequently, I have had a man on *On the Record* who really brings it all home. His name is Charles. Charles, who is in his sixties, worked for Enron for thirty years. He trusted the company and plowed all his savings into Enron's 401(k) retirement plan.

"Ma'am, we didn't have a clue. We didn't have a clue Enron was in trouble. We thought everything was lovey-dovey," Charles said.

He lost $1.4 million, his savings. And now Charles is fighting to survive.

"I get after tax $555.55 a month plus $1,294 Social Security. I have a mortgage payment $747.60 out of that. It's like stretching a rubber band. I am not living, just existing," he says.

Something is very wrong when this kind of thing can happen in America. The question, of course, is who is to blame?

Everyone is pointing fingers. Wall Street blames Congress, Congress blames Wall Street, the left blames capitalists, and the right blames Bill Clinton. Everybody blames greed, and almost nobody fesses up to having been greedy themselves. Some of my viewers—they can be a tough bunch—are even pointing fingers and blaming folks like Charles.

To: ontherecord@foxnews.com
From: Sheri in Lone Tree, Colorado

I have a great amount of sympathy for the Enron and World-Com employees who were on your show. The company execu-tives who caused these collapses to happen should be punished to the fullest extent of the law. However, investors also have responsibilities. All 401(k) plans have a variety of investment options, and diversification is imperative to protect yourself from losses such as these. Whenever you put that much money in one investment, no matter how good it looks, bad things can happen.

Sheri, it is hard for me to criticize an employee like Charles, who spent thirty years in the field working for Enron and then gets totally wiped out, when Ken Lay, who ran the company, has several Aspen properties.

12

AND NOW
A WORD FROM
OUR VIEWERS

A Collection of E-mails
from Viewers on Various Topics

To: ontherecord@foxnews.com
From: Bob in Fond du Lac, Wisconsin

I've loathed and detested Ozzy Osbourne and all that he sym-
bolized and appeared to stand for in the past. I've never enjoyed
his music (personal taste) and have never seen an episode of The
Osbournes. *After watching your interview with Ozzy and*
Sharon, I can honestly say I may have misjudged him. I found
him likeable and have a growing respect for the man. The idea
that he would be upset by the interview and wanting to sue over
it I find absurd. I'm just one of many (I assume) that have a
changing opinion (for the better) of Ozzy through this enjoyable
segment of On the Record. *Thank you for bringing this to us*
at the financial risk of a court case. I have to agree, the attorneys
are looking for a "deep pocket," not Ozzy's best interest.

Bob—thanks for your note. Ozzy is so different when
you talk to him or watch an interview than the years of
publicity about him. I really like Sharon and Ozzy. Also,

I don't believe they are upset, I think it is lawyers, and while I am one, I sometimes find them obnoxious! P.S.: Is Shreiner's restaurant still around? They had great banana cream pie. (I grew up in Appleton.)

Shreiner's restaurant is still thriving. The original owners sold it to a couple of the employees that worked their way up from dishwashers. Paul and Michael have owned it for a good ten years now and the quality of food and service has not diminished at all. Not only is the banana cream pie excellent as always, but the sticky bun (cinnamon roll) is out of this world (of course they serve it hot and with butter on the side, even though it is iced)—gotta love Wisconsin! I'm originally from western Michigan (Grand Rapids area) and have found the food here unlike anywhere else . . . ah, the dairy state. It was nice to hear back from you and enjoy the show tremendously. Honestly, I was a bit tentative about your coming to FNC after being with CNN and what your views were (again perceptions). I must admit, you challenge my views on many things. If you're ever back in the area, the banana cream pie is on my wife and me.

I just got back from a rained-out vacation to see your e-mail. I am delighted that Shreiner's is still there . . . and I love that the two former dishwashers now own it. However, I am starving right now and would kill for that banana cream pie, so I am going to send this message and go meet my husband for dinner! (Unfortunately, no pie!)

To: ontherecord@foxnews.com
From: Kevin in Webster, New Hampshire

I know I told you I wouldn't do this, but I can't let your last reply go without a brief response, so please indulge me this one last time. Take it for what it's worth from this thirty-year-old, I think you look absolutely amazing at forty-eight years young! I never would have guessed. Your honesty with me is as appreciated as your intellect. And don't chalk it all up to the minor work you had done; I know how humble you are about such things. In all respects, you're a very attractive girl, and that just helped to bring it out a little more so. Although I will say that since you've left that other network, I have noticed that the look of stress has completely left your face (gee, I wonder why?). Anyway, enjoy that new satellite radio—I hear John Mayer comes in pretty good on those things (ha ha). It should help to get the music flowing again (and what a big selection XM has!). Don't feel alone—I go through phases like that with music, too. Laura Ingraham didn't help in that department; now I never hear music on my way home from work. At least you have a good excuse, as being one of America's busiest women doesn't leave much time for anything else. Thank you for your sacrifice. You have been such a dear to write me back this many times, and I will cherish this always. But I will gracefully bow out now, I don't want to be one of those incessant e-mailers that you spoke of on Fox & Friends *back when you first arrived (good thing I was watching). You're so easy to talk to, and it's just way too easy to do. Coffee is on me the next time you're in New Hampshire. Stay safe this New Year's.*

Kevin—okay, I understand you are bowing out now from writing e-mails, but do keep watching.

To: ontherecord@foxnews.com
From: Brad in Clarksville, Tennessee

I am an avid viewer of the Fox News Channel. However, that will change after tonight's program. It is important to look back at news stories that affected the world in the past year; in doing so, it is my hope that history will not repeat itself. I was shocked and disgusted to see the vivid details of the victims of the Washington, D.C., sniper. The way in which you replayed video feeds from that nightmare was, in very nice terms, disgusting. Are your ratings worth subjecting the victims' families to the grief and horror they felt just a few months ago? Was it so necessary to show repeatedly the bloodshed (especially on the van and its surroundings) from their loved ones? Thank you for giving the individuals responsible for this horror exactly what they were looking for . . . attention. An apology to the victim's family is the least your network can provide.

I did not see the show, as it was one put together by the producers, but will say this: Realism makes people (including law enforcement) respond to important matters. Obviously this video made you mad, and I assume if we had another horrible crime spree like this you would not object to spending whatever time and resources to catch the criminals. I agree with you on this. I hope you keep watching, and from time to time we will have shows you love and shows you hate (but I hope the hate is rare). My staff is really working hard to do the best always.

To: ontherecord@foxnews.com
From: Susan in West Richland, Washington

Dear Greta: Thanks for your segment on rising malpractice costs, but please address the other issues that are strangling doctors. My husband has been an optometrist for almost nine years now and is very busy. But we are still barely making ends meet due to the shameful reimbursement by these same insurance companies that are charging outrageous sums for malpractice, and on the other end charging their subscribers obscene monthly premiums. We personally know two recent medical school graduates who are going into business instead of medicine for these same financial reasons. The upper administration makes many times what doctors can expect to make! Our largest insurer reimburses less than welfare! I have tried to address this but to no avail. And this is a company started by optometrists! Talk about forgetting your roots. In addition, the taxation on small businesses in our state is overwhelming. I have to work in the office because we cannot afford to pay another employee. I would be glad to provide you with more details if you have an interest in this subject. Thanks for all you do.

Susan—it is shameful how long it takes to get paid. And the amount of paperwork one must submit is insane as well. I agree with you.

To: ontherecord@foxnews.com
From: Zella in Louisville, Kentucky

I enjoy your program and watch it several times week, but I am really only writing to say that I liked your hair a bit blonder. It seems that lately it has a bit of ash tone and not a lot of style. It definitively adds something when you kick it up a notch and do yourself up a bit. I can tell you are a rather laid-back person when it comes to your look, and you opt for comfort and hygiene and not so much fluff. However, those of us who look at you every day appreciate the little things you do to make it enjoyable for us. Bless you and carry on!

You have me tagged right—I prefer comfort to fluff.

To: ontherecord@foxnews.com
From: Joe in Philadelphia, Pennsylvania

Good morning, Greta. How are you today? I thought I would write a compassionate e-mail to you today, in light of what happened on Saturday night in Green Bay. I don't have to consult with my intuition to know how you must feel about your favorite team. Honestly, I thought about you a lot in watching that game, and you must have wondered, as I did, that something is terribly wrong within the team and organization. I can remember an Atlanta Falcons player yesterday commenting on Green Bay yesterday on Fox Sports, saying that the Green Bay team had no fire in their eyes from the point of warming up to the execution of the game. You don't have to be a rocket scientist to know that changes are going to be made within the Green Bay organization, and if not, I will be very surprised. At any rate, it looks as though our bet is off due to circumstantial elimination. The Eagles will be playing the Falcons on Saturday night, so I guess we can give you satisfaction by ganging up on them Saturday night. I'll be there with a well-rested voice and plenty of energy. We're having a rally on Friday at one of our hangouts to get things started. Greta, this city is like a time bomb waiting to explode. I really regret our potential bet because I am coming to D.C. in May with my attorney to appear in appellate court. We could have stopped at Fox News to collect there after our victory in court.

It sure was a rotten game. You are right, I was not
pleased.

To: ontherecord@foxnews.com
From: Robert in Springfield, Illinois

*Dear Greta: You are the best news show on TV. I could not
watch you for over two minutes when you were on that other
news network. When Fox reported you were going to be on
their network as a host, I wondered what they were thinking of.
The only thing I can say now is, I was wrong. You have guests
on that no one else has and you ask questions that no one else
does. These questions are excellent questions. I guess that knew
where your true talent was. Keep up the excellent work. I'm an
avid viewer who has become addicted to your show.*

Robert, I am thrilled that you are "addicted." I am also
flattered. Many thanks.

To: ontherecord@foxnews.com
From: Judith in Texarkana, Arkansas/Texas

*Hey, Greta! Hope all is good your way and happy new year to
you and yours! I watch your show on occasion and really enjoy
it. Now—yesterday I was having my oil changed and tires
rotated. While sitting there waiting I picked up a* People *mag-*

azine, February's issue, I believe. Anyway, I was reading about the eye lift you had. Hell, I need a body lift . . . LOL! Well, as I was reading I was glad to see that this procedure you had done was because you wanted to and not really something you were expected to do to keep your ratings. :) BTW, you look great either way. :) Now, I have a question to this, because women are expected to look a certain way for the camera/viewers and such, where's the improvement to some of these butt-ugly anchormen? I mean, women like to look at a handsome man on the tube also! I see some bald/long in the face—I mean unattractive as heck! Just my opinion, by the way. Now, we know that men as they grow older seem to age better—nature has its unfair way of doing that—but that doesn't hold true for all men. Sooo, what's being done about that? I see nothing from here, and I guess it just goes to show that this is still a man's world when it comes to the workplace and who has a prettier face to be shown to the world— not referring to you—but I do know it does happen more than it should. As if our brains aren't enough. I'm talking about the average woman out there having and making the same match in occupation, at least those on tube/screen. I know this has been pondered in the past by many, but I see an unfair thing going on here and would like to see more Rogaine used, for starters. LOL! I just can't help myself when it comes to this issue. :) And don't get me started . . . LOL! Thanks for reading if you did and take care. :)

Judith—I am happy that *People* was there for you to read while your tires were rotated! (By the way, yesterday I spent hours getting my driver's license renewed!) Yes, this is still a male-dominated work world, but we are making gains!

To: ontherecord@foxnews.com
From: Jimmy in Nashville, Tennessee

I used to try to watch you on CNN, but because I got to the point that I couldn't stand it I quit. I felt that was so pointedly biased and that the anchors and show hosts (including you) were all from the same mold. When you first came on FNC I didn't want to watch your program because I felt it would be a liberal tilt without any objectivity and that it would be a repeat of the other. But I tried it, and lo and behold, your show is one of my favorites to watch on FNC. You give the most objective news reporting and news analysis on TV. I don't know what your politics are and it doesn't matter. All I know is that when I watch your show I feel I am seeing the true picture as it is being reported. Keep up the good work and stay the course. Whether you are liberal, moderate, or conservative I can't see it. You treat all your guests the same . . . with respect. You have earned mine.

Jimmy—many thanks. I appreciate that you gave me a chance and that you now are a regular viewer. I hope I don't disappoint you.

MY TURN AT THE BULLY PULPIT

To: ontherecord@foxnews.com
From: Elaine in West Springfield, Massachusetts

I was watching Hannity & Colmes, *and when they went to commercial, I flipped to CNN to see what the topic was. Well, they were talking about Laci Peterson. Someone called in and mentioned the drapes. It seems every day Laci used to open them in the morning, but this was not the case on December 24. This person said, "Why do we think Laci was alive on December 24?" Made me think. Only the dog was seen, or am I wrong? Was Laci seen on December 24 or just their dog? She could have disappeared the night before. Something to think about. As far as Saddam is concerned, he has to go one way or another.*

Elaine—why were you flipping to CNN? I hope you watch my show.

Now, now, Greta. I watch and/or listen to FNC only. Glad you're not at CNN anymore. Made you look as though you were leaning one way only. Liked Paula Zahn, but you are so, so much better. Never miss your show unless the Red Sox are having a night game and it's being televised. Hey, I love my Sox. I know, they're not the best team, but I always stand by them.

Oh, good! I was worried you were watching the competition! I don't blame you for watching the Sox!

Technically, CNN isn't even competition with FNC. See you tonight.

Great . . . don't be late! I can't be late or I will be in big trouble!

To: ontherecord@foxnews.com
From: Carol in Provo, Utah

Just wanted Greta and Fox News to know that she is my career idol and I have been totally impressed as I have watched her career. How many people could make the transition from lawyer to hard-hitting newsie? Go girl! I should confess I am really conservative, so I was dubious: is she . . . isn't she . . . Well, I still can't tell! But that's okay because she's fair and that's all I could or should ask. I always enjoy watching OTR. Go Fox News!

Carol—I am very flattered by your note. I hope you keep watching.

To: ontherecord@foxnews.com
From: Becky in Fort Worth, Texas

I am in the process of looking for a plastic surgeon to perform eye surgery. I realize there are many to choose from; however, I would like some personal recommendations. Would it be possible to give me the name of the person who performed your eyelid cosmetic surgery? Thanking you in advance for your help.

Becky—when I had my eyes done, it became a huge media circus. I had not dreamed it would be of any interest to anyone. I went public because I did not see the big deal in having it done, but now I fear that if I reveal my doctor's name, the media will camp out at his office and hound the many men and women who get plastic surgery and want to do so discreetly. I told the doctor I don't care if he outs himself, but that I would respect him and not do so. Having said this, the procedure I had done is not unusual and many doctors do it. I suggest you visit three plastic surgeons and interview each as to what he/she can do/cannot do and make a decision.

To: ontherecord@foxnews.com
From: Marvin in Gainesville, Florida

Greta, I love how you went from TV analyst in the OJ case to having your own show, awesome! Twenty-four years a cop, fifteen as a detective and internal affairs investigator—I enjoy what you do in these high-profile criminal cases. Like Peterson didn't kill Laci? Furman is also awesome and you can tell him I said so. He was a great detective and it wasn't his fault the criminal case on Orenthal went south. I just wish he would have come out and testified he said that infamous word. I have said it. So? But the man knows his stuff—I would have loved working cases with him, and he knows damn well as everyone else, Markie Poo is in big doo-doo! You are sharp, I love your questions, and you must have been awesome in court! I give the Laci case a few more days and Markie will be changing his name to Ben. I am sure you know the last name, I won't be writtenly crude. Sick society we live in, and the world in general. I am not religious but there are way too many signs that if people don't get their s*** together soon, the big guy may take it all away. What he giveth he can taketh away! I send O'Reilly e-mails on occasion, one tonight, including the e-mail I sent to the school board outside St. Louis that voted to let the sick puppy chaperone schoolkids. What next, Lester Molester leading a Brownie troop, or Father O'Quinn being a Cub Scout leader? I am definitely a right-wing conservative and love your show. The entire Fox News Channel is by far the most accurate and nonbiased on the tube. And . . . you look great too! Keep it up!

Marvin—twenty-four years as a cop? Wow! I bet you know your stuff when it comes to these investigations. I appreciate you watching and writing.

To: ontherecord@foxnews.com
From: Tom in Greeneville, Tennessee
Subject: Inyerview

Good interview of Muhammad's neighbor. Many more like that and your rating will be number .1.

Good job spelling *interview.*

You know, that's the first smart remark I've received from any professional organization. I'm just disappointed it was from Fox.

You earned that remark.

I'm sorry, but I have to make an observation here. I did make a curt remark about an interview Greta did with Muhammad's neighbor which should have been over with the first question. I couldn't believe a producer would set her up like that. It had to be embarrassing for her. Now, I did make a short cute curt remark about it. I agree. However, all the response was about was spelling. Well, I guess spell-check doesn't check the subject line. I'm not the world's best speller or typist. You see, on the keyboard the letter Y and T are next to each other. The correction was okay. The lack of a response was missing about the interview. Fox is my network and will continue to be so. But you guys have to be able to put up with tactful assholes like me and respond to the statement, not just the grammar or spelling. I guess I'm just a little cynical about most things these days. Anyway, keep up the good work. P.S. I looked this one over reallllllly good. Most likely a C-.

Tom—I was just having a little fun, as I assumed you were, too. I actually appreciate you writing the show, and I appreciate you watching. Yes, that interview was horrible! Best, Greta.

Wow, that was you all the time? I thought I was talking with someone else. I'm honored you could take the time. Enough already with inyerview. *Thanks for the response and I'll be watching with adjusted vigor.*

Tom—I am thrilled you will watch. I love being at Fox.

MY TURN AT THE BULLY PULPIT

To: ontherecord@foxnews.com
From: Pattyann in Pennsburg, Pennsylvania

Great show, as usual, last night. I know you are a lawyer so please don't take this personally. My husband and I agree with the doc from West Virginia. We feel the judges certainly shouldn't be allowing half the cases to come to trial. It all starts there. Something needs to be done to stop the mayhem because we are all paying for it. Thanks for listening!

Pattyann—I agree with you. Judges *must* do their jobs. If a frivolous lawsuit is filed, a judge should on day one throw it out. The judge in most jurisdictions can also penalize the lawyer filing it.

To: ontherecord@foxnews.com
From: Cheryl in Mansfield, Texas

Gretta, for months now my three-and-a-half-year-old daughter, Clara Marie, has been a huge fan of yours! It all started when we were sitting down to unwind and watch a few minutes of Fox News Channel at bedtime one night and your show was on. She started asking what your name was and now you are part of our nightly routine. Hardly a week night goes by that we don't sit down to "watch Gretta" for at least a few minutes. She's watched so much lately, she even knows Bernie Grimm's name! Now that's a little scary! And when she hears your voice on the On the Record *spots on other shows, she shouts, "Gretta!" even though your picture isn't even on the screen.*

She's always very interested in the show and always asks questions like "Why is she on every day?" (Laci), "What's his name?" or "What's her name?" about your guests, and she always wonders why you're outside, or why you were in that tank the other night, etc., when you're not in the studio.

I just thought you should know you have a really big little fan out here in Texas! I'm attaching a couple of shots of her watching the show—hope they give you a chuckle! I love your show, too, but can't come close to Clara! Have a great weekend! See you tonight!

Greta—I was horrified when I watched the show the next time and realized you only have one t *in your name. I hate it when people spell my name(s) wrong (it happens all the time) and I'm sure you do too. Sorry! Please don't hold it against Clara! So far she only knows how to spell* her *name.*

Cheryl—don't worry about it! My mother used to slip and call me by the cat's name, so having my name wrongly spelled is minor!

MY TURN AT THE BULLY PULPIT

To: ontherecord@foxnews.com
From: Alan in Las Vegas, Nevada

Yesterday I picked up Rush Limbaugh's replay of the know-nothing Tacoma neighbor of Muhammad who you interviewed the other day. I'm sure that that interview was a real embarrassment to you. However, you have got to know it was very, very funny! I almost lost control of my car laughing. It was sort of reminiscent of some of the Johnny Carson deadhead interviews. If you haven't laughed about it yet, go back and look at it again. This may not seem funny now, in a few years, you will reflect upon this very humbling moment with a smile.

For many years we had a miniature schnauzer, Max, who got into the habit of howling when the alarm clock went off. I soon discovered that he would also howl on cue if I howled first. He was clearly stupid pet trick material. One Saturday afternoon somebody, I don't recall who, sponsored a stupid pet trick contest at a local shopping center. There were hundreds in attendance and the contest was judged by a district court judge, a city councilman, and a TV weatherman. I decided to take Max and enter the contest. We had practiced and had it down perfect. I really thought that we might win. I would start Max off by howling myself and then he would join in with his high-pitched wail. God knows how long he would go on with that. Sometimes he would howl for five minutes or more! We decided to call our act the "Barbra Streisand and Donna Summer duet."

Saturday arrived and our turn came. I felt that we were a

cinch to win or at least place. We had a very funny act. Little did I know.

I announced our act and then started to howl. Max stood there and did nothing. I howled again; Max stood there and did nothing. I was beginning to get embarrassed. I decided to howl longer and louder. I'm not sure if it was on that howl or the next that I visualized the still silent Max giving me the finger. The judges and the audience were hysterical. As we slunk off the stage, I got the realization that we might not win.

Back then I was embarrassed. Today I look at it as a fond memory of my friend Max.

I love Max! What a hoot. I can't believe he did that to you! As for the interview, you are right, it was so bad that it was very funny!

To: ontherecord@foxnews.com
From: Mildred in Lucas (Dallas), Texas

Hello, Greta: I have a brother, Archie, who came home today from his tour on the USS Teddy Roosevelt. The majority of his immediate family live down south in Baton Rouge and Dallas and were unable to meet him in Virginia. Of course we are sad about this, more so after seeing the tearful and joyful reunions of families that were able to met their Navy men this morning. If at all possible, upon closing your show tonight, could you please mention his name and say how much we love him and how extremely proud we all are of him and the other Navy sailors? Thank you.

Millie—I have passed this request on to my producers. Cross your fingers that we can slip it into the show.

Greta: I'd like to take this moment to thank you and the show for allowing my request to be broadcast. This was so kind of you to pass it on—I sincerely appreciate it.

Laugh time—my husband and I used to religiously watch this certain cable television evening talk show hosted by a well-known legal expert. We noticed that the host(ess?) of that show wasn't around at Christmas time—we figured she was on vacation. When she didn't appear around New Year's, I e-mailed this network to inquire "Where is Greta—surely she can't be on vacation this long? Is she traveling abroad?" Days later, I finally got an e-mail reply back from CNN that said, "Thank you for your interest in The Point. *However, due to increased volume of e-mails, we can't answer all inquiries." Ha ha ha ha ha. Then this same reply got "stuck" some kind of way in computer land and I was sent this same response almost every hour for that entire workday. It was so funny. We like your new Fox show and we also enjoyed you on* The Point. *Similar to President Clinton, you have this knack of appearing relaxed and being able to comfortably interview all walks of life, from dignitaries and exalted foreign leaders to rap artists fresh out of prison.*

Thank you again.

About the Authors

GRETA VAN SUSTEREN is host of *On the Record with Greta Van Susteren* on the Fox News Channel. Prior to her television career she was an attorney and adjunct professor of law at Georgetown University. She writes a monthly column for *Men's Health* and lives in the Washington, D.C., area.

ELAINE LAFFERTY is the Editor in Chief of *Ms.* magazine. She is a highly respected journalist and foreign correspondent who has written for many publications, including *Time, The Nation,* and *The Irish Times.*